Where God Wants You to Be

A Call to Missions

Charles E. Cravey

In His Steps Publishing

Copyright © 2025 by Charles Edward Cravey

All rights reserved.

You may not reproduce any portion of this book in any form without written permission from the publisher or author, except as permitted by U.S. copyright law.

All scripture is from the King James Version of the Bible.

ISBN: 978-1-58535-037-7 (PRINT)

ISBN: 978-1-58535-040-7 (KINDLE) EPUB

Library of Congress Catalog Number: 2025905294

Cover designed by Charles E. Cravey and Bookbrush

Contents

Foreword	V
Dedication	VII
Introduction	IX
1. Where God Wants You to Be	1
2. Why Do We Go?	25
3. The Faces of the Children	37
4. Ecuador's Guinea Pig Feast	45
5. Something Greater than Ourselves	49
6. Missions at Home	57
7. Our Venezuela Encounter	64
8. Katrina's Mission	71
9. The Missionary Named Paul	78

10.	Modern Echoes of Paul's Journeys	88
11.	Ole Henry and Ahmed	93
12.	Faith and Missions	99
13.	"Unto the Least" - Rev. Bobby Gale	107
14.	"One Small Step for Man"	112
15.	A Call to Mission	121
16.	A Seed of Hope	123
17.	In Memoriam: Jamie Gibson	125

Foreword

It is a profound honor to write this foreword for my dear friend and mentor, Rev. Dr. Charles Cravey. Charles has helped to shape my love for mission and deepen my walk with God. His wisdom, encouragement, and unwavering faith played a crucial role in my development, guiding me through moments of discernment and action.

Our journeys together with Volunteers in Mission to Central America, the Caribbean disaster relief, and recoveries were more than just trips—they were transformative experiences where I witnessed Charles putting Christ's love into action. He didn't just preach the gospel; he lived it, serving with a heart full of compassion and a spirit of humility. His dedication to missions and his ability to inspire those around him are testaments to a life fully surrendered to God's calling.

Charles and his wife, Renee, embody the essence of servant leadership, demonstrating that faith is not just something we believe, but something we do. His influence has left an indelible mark on my life, and I am forever grateful for his guidance and friendship.

May the words in this book reflect the heart of a man who has truly walked the path of God's love, service, and unwavering faith.

Rev. Bobby Gale

Unto the Least of His Ministry

Dedicated to my Wonderful Pastors:

Rev. Lauren West

and

Rev. Mark Burgess

Introduction

I had never once envisioned embarking on a foreign mission, much less soaring through the skies on an airplane! Yet the Divine had grander designs for my service than merely tending to a local flock. The more I sought to evade the call of missions, the more it pursued me. When God whispers your name, He will not rest until you heed His call.

That sacred summons reached me in 1980, when a dear friend and fellow minister implored me to join an upcoming mission journey to the enchanting lands of Costa Rica. With my guitar in hand and a voice ready to sing, he envisioned my role as the melodic heart of both team gatherings and church worship services. I swiftly suggested several other ministers who could strum an instrument and lift their voices, but he refused to accept my reluctance! For weeks, he would ring me with unwavering persistence, and each time, my answer remained a resolute no.

To succinctly weave the tale, divine providence swept away my hesitations, urging me forth on a journey of purpose! Miraculously, anonymous gifts paved the way for my adventure, a testament to my role in 'His' grand mission—details to unfold later within these pages.

I vividly recall clutching the armrests of my airplane seat, whispering prayers throughout the ascent from Hartsfield International Airport in Atlanta. Moments later, I dared to peek through the tiny porthole, and a sea of clouds enveloped us as we soared. Then came a serene tranquility as the plane leveled, revealing the most resplendent clouds I had ever beheld! In that instant, it felt as though God was cradling my hand, offering solace, and assuring me He was in command, and all was well.

From that transformative moment onward, I relinquished control over my life, surrendering completely to God! It marked the dawn of my inaugural mission trip, yet it would not be the last. That first journey awakened a profound understanding within me: faith transcends borders and languages, manifesting in the shared humanity and unwavering hope of those I met. The lessons I learned from the people of Costa Rica—about resilience, grace, and the beauty of humble faith—reshaped my perspective, reminding me that every soul carries a story worth cherishing.

I diligently set aside funds each month, aspiring to embark on at least one foreign journey annually. I immersed myself in local mission endeavors—hurricane and tornado relief, soup kitchens, food banks, and shelters. A fervent fire ignited within my heart, one that would never extinguish but only blaze brighter with each expedition, each experience, and every adventure encountered. I felt vibrantly alive, even at 73.

After sixty-eight foreign missions, I primarily remain within the borders of my homeland, channeling my gifts into local missions and supporting noble causes. Yet, my passion burns as brightly now as it did forty-five years ago. Each night, the faces of children from distant lands grace my thoughts, and I pray for fellow mission workers laboring in the fields of Africa or ministers standing on bare earthen floors, proclaiming the word of God beneath tattered tents. I beseech the will of God to summon more laborers to the harvest.

'The fields stand abundant for the harvest, yet the laborers are but a scarce few.' It is my fervent prayer that this work will send out a call to you, my fellow laborer, to give yourself to the call of God for missions, be it here at home or abroad. Whether you find yourself drawn to the bustling streets of a distant city or the quiet corners of your own neighborhood, know that every minor act of kindness and service contributes to a greater tapestry of love and compassion. Embrace the opportunity to share your unique gifts, for each of us has a role to play in this divine mission.

Consider how you might use your talents—whether in music, teaching, building, or simply offering a listening ear—to make a difference in the lives of those around you. Remember, grand gestures or fanfare don't always accompany the call to serve.

May you have meaningful encounters on your journey, and may you shine as a beacon of hope and light wherever you go. Let us join hands in this beautiful endeavor, trusting that together we can sow seeds of peace and joy that will flourish across the world.

Charles E. Cravey, March 2025

1

Where God Wants You to Be

We soared into Georgetown, Guyana, with hearts brimming with anticipation, only to be ushered to a humble dormitory, a relic of the Methodist Church's endeavors from fifty years past to host mission teams. The weather greeted us with unkindness! The heat was relentless, and the air clung to us like a warm embrace. Here, we would rest for the night, preparing to embark on a boat the next morning for a captivating day-trip upriver to the quaint village where our mission work awaited. Nestled among the church families, we would pair up, weaving our lives into the fabric of their community.

Throughout the night, relentless mosquitoes tormented us, transforming our dorm stay into a wretched ordeal. With only fragile sheets to shield our bodies, we found little solace from their incessant bites. I vividly recall the restless dance of twisting and turning, barely grasping an hour or two of fleeting sleep.

As dawn broke, the symphony of the jungle came alive, offering a gentle reprieve from the night's challenges. The air was cooler, and the sky painted itself in hues of pink and orange, promising a fresh beginning. We gathered our belongings and spirits, ready to embrace the adventure that lay ahead.

The boat awaited us, a modest vessel bobbing gently against the dock. As we climbed aboard, the excitement of the day washed away the discomfort of the night. The river stretched out before us like a ribbon of possibilities, its calm surface reflecting the dense greenery that lined its banks.

As we journeyed upriver, the landscape unfolded in a vibrant tapestry of life. The sounds of the jungle accompanied us—a chorus of birds, the rustle of leaves, and the distant calls of unseen creatures. Along the way, our guide shared stories of the land and its people, weaving a rich narrative that deepened our appreciation for the place we were about to visit.

Because of the boat's tardy arrival, we endeavored to navigate the morning tide upriver, yet halfway to our village, our vessel ran aground and refused to budge! There we sat, enveloped by the jungle's embrace, with the sun blazing above and mosquitoes feasting upon our flesh, feeling utterly wretched. It would be two hours before the tides returned, lifting our boat back into the embrace of the water, allowing us to journey onward. Amidst the vibrant foliage, howler monkeys swung in the treetops along the banks, while the vivid hues of macaws, parakeets, and other wondrous wildlife captivated our weary hearts. We asked each other if we were in the right place, and the old missionary with us kept reminding us we were where God wanted us.

Reaching the village felt like stepping into a storybook. The community greeted us with warmth and open arms, their smiles as bright as the morning sun. Children laughed and played, their joy infectious, while the adults welcomed us into their homes and hearts. Here, amidst the simplicity and beauty of their lives, we found a sense of purpose and connection that transcended the trials of our journey. We were indeed "where God wanted us to be!"

As twilight descended, my companion and I found ourselves gently set down at the terminus of a winding dirt path, instructed to traverse with our flashlights toward the first dwelling on the left. Burdened with our luggage and a box of mission supplies each, we approached our destination. We encountered a delightful couple and their three children there; they greeted us warmly and hospitably. They offered us refreshing fruit juice, enveloping us in the welcoming embrace of their modest sanctuary.

Following warm pleasantries and an explanation of our mission to the couple, they ushered us to our cozy upstairs bedroom, furnished with the essentials of comfort. An inviting open window welcomed us, allowing the melody of buzzing mosquitoes to fill the air. Gratefully, the family had kindled mosquito burners in our sanctuary, a thoughtful gesture to ward off the pesky intruders! For the next eight days, we would share this abode with them, forging bonds of camaraderie. Just beyond our door lay a charming balcony, where we could bask in the embrace of the morning sun, sipping our coffee as we prepared to embark on our journey to the mission site.

As the golden sun began its ascent over the verdant jungle horizon, my friend and I stirred from our snug double bed, a cozy nest that barely afforded us the space to turn! Downstairs, a steaming cup of coffee awaited, prompting us to hastily splash ourselves with water from a basin, attend to our morning rituals, and rush downstairs to savor a lovingly prepared breakfast of guava, mangoes, bananas, and scrambled eggs fresh from the family's chickens.

For me, the coffee was a divine elixir—homegrown, dark, and rich, exactly as I adore. My friend delighted in the fruit juice, praising its exquisite flavor. With our juice and coffee in hand, we retreated upstairs to gather our materials for the day's endeavors at the mission. Perched on the balcony, we soaked in the sunrise as a vibrant flock of macaws swooped into the nearby trees. Their resplendent hues captivated the eyes, though their raucous squawks pierced the morning tranquility!

As we gathered around the breakfast table, a foreboding tale graced our ears about the creek that meandered into their camp. The story of anacondas in the creek, especially the tale of a tiny three-year-old boy swept away and vanished without a trace, sent shivers down our spines. This chilling revelation instilled a deep sense of dread in both my friend and me as we pondered such formidable beings in our midst.

Despite the ominous tale, the warmth of our hosts and the vibrant energy of the village rekindled our spirits. We couldn't let fear overshadow the purpose that had brought us here. Determined to make a positive impact, we prepared to head to the mission site, armed with our supplies and a newfound resolve.

The path to the mission was a winding trail through the jungle, where the dappled sunlight filtered through the thick canopy above. As we walked, the sounds of the village faded, replaced by the symphony of the forest. Every step brought us closer to our destination, but also deeper into the heart of this wild, untamed landscape.

At the mission site, eager faces, both young and old, who had gathered to see what we offered, greeted us. The children's laughter was infectious, and their curiosity about our work was clear in their wide eyes and endless questions. It was here, amidst the vibrant chaos, that we realized the true power of connection. Language barriers dissolved in the face of genuine smiles and shared goals.

Throughout the day, we painted, repaired, and built alongside the villagers, each task a testament to the strength of community. The sun beat down relentlessly, but our determination never wavered. With every brushstroke and hammer swing, we felt the ties between us and the villagers grow stronger.

At the zenith of the day, we guided a Vacation Bible School class for fifty eager young hearts, a delightful endeavor that would unfold over five sunlit days. On the following Sunday, the children would joyfully share the treasures of wisdom they had gathered during their time at school in the sacred worship services. In a joyful interlude one afternoon, we ventured to the shimmering beachfront to engage in spirited soccer matches with the children, basking in the warmth of camaraderie and laughter following Bible School.

In that evocative backdrop, we discovered that Jonestown, the notorious enclave forged by the Rev. Jim Jones, lay mere miles from our temporary haven. A kind gentleman of the community regaled us with tales, portraying the denizens of Jonestown as gentle souls, overflowing with warmth and affection. He expressed disbelief at the tragic events that unfolded there, with the haunting specter of mass suicides casting a long shadow over their legacy.

As evening approached, the sky transformed into a canvas of purples and oranges, signaling the end of our first day at the mission. Exhausted but fulfilled, we made our way back to our hosts' home, our hearts full of the knowledge that we had made a difference.

That night, as we lay in our cozy room, the sounds of the jungle serenaded us into a peaceful slumber. The tales of anacondas and other lurking dangers seemed a world away, overshadowed by the warmth and unity we had found. Here, in this remote corner of the world, we discovered that the most powerful force was not fear but love and community.

It had also been a triumphant day in the realm of our building endeavor. We toiled under the sun, laying concrete block walls and mixing mortar, the essence of our labor imbued with sweat and determination. Though the work proved arduous for many, each team member embraced the challenge, often seeking refuge in the shade to catch their breath. I vividly recall when one brave soul let out a piercing shriek, for as she reclined against a palm tree, succumbing to a brief slumber, a tarantula made its bold ascent up her clothing, finding its perch upon her neck! Jamie would forever carry the echoes of that startling encounter! Despite the surprise, laughter quickly followed, easing the tension and reinforcing the camaraderie among us. Moments like these, though unexpected, bonded us even more, turning potential fears into shared stories that would be told and retold with fondness.

As the sun dipped lower, casting long shadows across our worksite, we took a step back to admire the fruits of our labor. The walls stood tall and proud, a testament not only to our physical efforts but to the unity and perseverance that had brought us this far. It was more than just a building; it was a symbol of hope and progress for the community we cherished.

Evening descended with a gentle breeze, a welcome reprieve from the day's heat. We gathered around a makeshift table for dinner, sharing stories, laughter, and a meal lovingly prepared by our hosts. The simple yet flavorful dishes spoke of the region's rich culture, and every bite was a reminder of the kindness and hospitality that had enveloped us since our arrival.

As the stars twinkled in the vast sky above, we sat together, reflecting on the day's triumphs and challenges. There was a profound sense of fulfillment in knowing that our efforts were not just constructing walls, but building bridges of friendship and understanding. It was in these quiet moments, under the watchful gaze of the moon and the symphony of nocturnal creatures, that we truly felt the impact of our mission.

With hearts full of gratitude and anticipation for the days to come, we retired to our rooms, ready to embrace the adventures that awaited us on the morrow. Here, in this corner of the world, far from the comforts of home, we learned that the most valuable lessons came not from textbooks, but from the heart. The words also echoed from our old missionary friend: "You are exactly where God wants you to be!"

As dawn's gentle light kissed the horizon, we ventured down the following morning to cleanse ourselves at a communal faucet fed by the crystalline waters of the creek below. The liquid was icy, sending shivers through our very souls, yet the call to bathe was undeniable. Thus, my friend and I bravely embraced the chill, dousing ourselves in the frigid embrace of nature! It was here, by the creek's edge, that whispers of the anaconda sighting lingered, and where the little boy had bravely ventured forth. We couldn't help but feel a mix of awe and apprehension, knowing the stories that surrounded this serene yet mysterious place. The water, despite its chill, invigorated us and washed away the remnants of sleep, readying us for another day of meaningful work and connection.

After our brisk morning ritual, we joined the village for a hearty breakfast. The meal was a simple yet delicious affair, with fresh eggs, tropical fruits, and warm bread that filled us with energy and warmth. The villagers, ever gracious and welcoming, shared stories and laughter, easing any lingering fears with their genuine kindness.

As we prepared to head back to the mission site, the morning sun filtered through the trees, casting dappled shadows on the ground. The path seemed more familiar now, each step a testament to the bonds we were forging and the lives we were touching.

We had varied tasks for the day—some of us continued construction, laying more bricks, and mixing mortar, while others assisted in teaching and playing with the children. Every moment spent in this vibrant community felt precious, each interaction a reminder of the shared humanity that connected us all.

In the afternoon, a refreshing breeze swept through the village, offering relief from the heat, and energizing our spirits. We took a moment to rest, sitting together in the shade, sharing stories and dreams, and reflecting on the journey that had brought us here.

As the day drew to a close, we gathered once more with our hosts, exchanging tales of the day's adventures over a delightful dinner. Their warmth and hospitality continued to envelop us, making this faraway place feel like home.

Under the starry sky, with the jungle's symphony as our lullaby, we retired for the night, grateful for the experiences and friendships that were blossoming. Here, amidst the beauty and challenges of this remote village, we were discovering the profound impact of love, community, and purpose. As we drifted into sleep, the words of our old missionary friend resonated in our hearts: "You are exactly where God wants you to be."

As dawn broke and we embarked on our journey to the worksite, our third day unfolded with a delightful surprise; children awaited us at the lane's end, eagerly joining us for the stroll to the church building. With hands clasped and materials in tow, they embraced us as if we were kindred spirits from ages past. Their joyous laughter illuminated the path, wrapping Jim and me in a warm embrace, making us feel as though we had truly come home.

I devoted the day to adorning the windows flanking the new sanctuary, striving to coax the crooked boards into alignment! The wise old missionary shared that, under the sun's fiery gaze, the boards would bend, requiring careful manipulation to restore their straightness.

Despite the challenge, I found a certain rhythm in the work, each nail I drove and each board I adjusted feeling like a step toward bringing the community's vision to life. The children watched with fascination, occasionally offering a helping hand or a word of encouragement that lifted my spirits.

As the day progressed, the sun's heat intensified, but the camaraderie and shared purpose made the labor feel lighter. During a brief break, I sat with the children under the shade of a large tree, where they shared stories and songs that spoke of their lives and dreams. Their laughter was infectious, a reminder of the joy and resilience that thrived in this small village. Most of the boys aspired to be professional soccer players, yet the challenge loomed large, for achieving this dream in the depths of the Amazonian jungle would prove quite formidable.

By late afternoon, the windows stood proudly, their frames perfectly aligned, ready to welcome the light of countless sunrises and the warmth of community gatherings. The satisfaction of seeing the sanctuary take shape was immeasurable, knowing that it would soon be a place of worship and refuge for all who entered.

As the sun dipped below the horizon, painting the sky with hues of gold and pink, we gathered with the villagers to celebrate the day's achievements. A feast awaited us, a delicious array of local dishes that filled the air with tantalizing aromas. We shared stories and laughter, our hearts full of gratitude for the connections we were forging. The villagers had lovingly roasted a pig in a deep earthen pit throughout the day, and it was utterly divine! This marked the first taste of meat we savored on our adventure, and every member of the team relished it with joyous abandon.

That evening, as I lay in bed, the sounds of the jungle lulled me into a restful sleep. The day's efforts had not only strengthened the physical structure of the sanctuary but also deepened the bonds between us all. Here, amidst the beauty and simplicity of the village, I truly felt something greater at work—a divine purpose guiding us every step of the way.

In the days to come, I knew there would be more challenges and triumphs, but with each one, we would continue to build not just walls, but a community bound by love and faith.

The following day, I embarked on the noble task of crafting wooden pews from a design shared by a kindred missioner. The plan was straightforward yet effective. It consumed much of my day, but the satisfaction was profound.

Mid-morning, we once again gathered the children for lessons until the hour of lunch. I strummed my guitar and sang melodies that brought joy to their eager hearts. Melodies like "Jesus Loves Me" and "Kum-ba-ya" resonated through the lush embrace of the jungle. The children's voices joined in with enthusiasm, their laughter and joy mingling with the music, creating a harmony that transcended language and culture. In those moments, the jungle seemed to sway with us, the leaves rustling as if in applause.

After our musical interlude, we transitioned into the lessons for the day. Their eager eyes and curious questions made teaching an absolute delight. We explored stories from the Bible, each tale coming alive with the children's vivid imaginations and boundless creativity.

As the sun climbed higher, the village bustled with activity. Some of the team members worked tirelessly on the construction site, while others engaged with the villagers, learning their crafts and sharing stories. The bonds we were forming felt like a tapestry, intricately woven with threads of friendship, understanding, and shared purpose.

Lunchtime brought us together once more, a communal gathering that reinforced the sense of belonging. The meals were simple yet nourishing, prepared with love and care. Each bite was a testament to the hospitality and warmth that enveloped us.

Everyone dedicated the afternoon to more construction work, helping to build the sanctuary. The sound of hammers and saws filled the air, accompanied by the cheerful chatter of those working side by side. It was a symphony of productivity and unity.

As the day's work ended, we admired the progress we had made. The sanctuary was becoming a reality, each brick and beam a testament to the collaboration and dedication that defined our mission.

Evening descended gently, bringing with it a sense of accomplishment and peace. We gathered for dinner, sharing stories of the day's adventures and marveling at the beauty of the star-studded sky above. The villagers' warmth and generosity continued to embrace us, making this distant place feel like home.

As we settled in for the night, the jungle's nocturnal symphony serenaded us to sleep. Our hearts were full, knowing that our efforts were making a meaningful difference, not only in the physical structures we were building, but in the lives we were touching.

In the days to come, we would continue to work, learn, and grow alongside this vibrant community, discovering that the most profound lessons came not from the tasks we completed, but from the connections we forged. Here, in this corner of the world, amidst the challenges and triumphs, we were truly where God wanted us to be.

On Thursday evening, we gathered for a sacred worship service within the embrace of the new church building's hull. Above us, the stars twinkled with celestial brilliance, and the spirit of God danced among our hearts. With my guitar in hand, I joined forces with the team to guide the congregation in a harmonious celebration of our cherished hymns. The melodies filled the air, their notes weaving a tapestry of hope and gratitude that resonated deep within our souls. As voices rose in unison, a profound sense of unity enveloped us, transcending the boundaries of our distinct cultures. Each hymn was a testament to the strength and resilience of the community, a shared expression of faith that had carried us through challenges and triumphs alike.

The villagers' fervent voices mingled with ours, creating a symphony that echoed through the trees, a reminder of the divine presence that had guided us throughout our journey. Gentle shadows, cast by the flickering candlelight on the walls, symbolized the light we had kindled in our hearts.

As the service ended, we gathered in a circle, hand in hand, offering prayers of thanksgiving for the experiences and connections that had enriched our lives. The warmth of the villagers' smiles and the sincerity in their eyes reaffirmed the purpose that had brought us here.

In those muted moments, surrounded by the beauty of the jungle and the love of newfound friends, we felt a profound sense of peace and fulfillment. The words of our old missionary friend echoed in our minds once more: "You are exactly where God wants you to be." It was a sacred affirmation of the journey we were on, a journey not just of building physical structures, but of nurturing the soul and spirit of community.

As we made our way back to our hosts' home, the night's gentle breeze carried with it the promise of new beginnings and continued growth. The bonds we had forged would remain long after our departure, a testament to the enduring power of love and shared purpose. And as we drifted into sleep, the jungle serenading us with its nocturnal symphony; we knew that this mission had truly been a blessing in every sense. I even felt that our missioners had received much more than we had given!

On Thursday morning, three fellow missioners and I embarked on the noble task of crafting the rafters for the roof, while others diligently fashioned double doors for the grand front entrance. After skillfully completing and securing the rafters atop rickety, sturdy tree limb ladders, we began installing the gleaming metal roof that had journeyed upriver from Georgetown. To our astonishment, the very day we would crown our creation with the roof, the metal had arrived early that morning! Truly, we saw divine providence in our endeavor!

As we affixed the last sheets of metal, a sense of accomplishment and gratitude swelled within us. The roof stood as a symbol of our shared commitment and hard work, a protective canopy under which the community would gather for years to come. The villagers cheered and applauded our efforts; their joy was evident in their bright smiles and appreciative gestures.

Once the roof was securely in place, we took a moment to step back and admire the fruits of our labor. The church, now complete with its sturdy roof, stood as a beacon of hope and unity in the village's heart. Our work, the church, stood as a testament not only to our physical accomplishments but also to the bonds we formed and the love we poured into every nail and beam.

Celebrations and preparations for the evening's worship service filled the rest of the day. Villagers gathered around, bringing with them vibrant flowers and handmade decorations to adorn the newly completed church. Excitement and anticipation filled the air, as the community shared a recognition of this moment's importance.

As the sun began to set, casting a warm glow over the village, we joined our hosts for a communal feast. The meal was a joyful affair, filled with laughter, stories, and a deep sense of connection. It was a celebration not just of the building itself, but of the journey we had all undertaken together.

That evening, the community gathered within the walls of the new church, their voices lifted in prayer and song. The sound echoed through the jungle, a joyful proclamation of faith and gratitude. As I played my guitar, leading the congregation in hymns, I felt a profound sense of peace and fulfillment. We were exactly where we were meant to be, surrounded by love and a shared purpose.

As the service came to a close, we stood together, hand in hand, offering prayers of thanksgiving for the journey that had brought us here. The stars above seemed to shine a little brighter, as if joining in our celebration. In those moments, we knew that this mission had been a blessing in every sense, a testament to the power of community, faith, and the divine guidance that had led us every step of the way.

With the church's completion unfolding in such swift grace, we revered God's handiwork. Each missioner united with fellow villagers, offering heartfelt thanks on our last day among these cherished people. That night, as the altar call echoed through the sacred space, thirty-five children filled us with wonder as they stepped forward, dedicating their lives to Christ! Thirty-five radiant souls embraced by the kingdom of God! What a magnificent moment to share in unity. These young hearts would carry forth the light, nurturing their community with a spirit of love and faith. Some may even embark on journeys as ministers, spreading the love of Christ far and wide, just as we had done.

As the last notes of the altar call faded into the night, a profound sense of fulfillment and joy enveloped us all. The villagers gathered around the children, enveloping them in warm embraces and words of encouragement. It was a moment of celebration, not just for the commitments made, but for the promise of hope and transformation that each child represented.

The evening unfolded with a spirit of gratitude and fellowship. Friends, old and new, shared stories of the past days, laughed, and whispered plans. The bonds we had formed over the eight days felt unbreakable, woven together with threads of shared experiences and mutual respect.

As the night sky deepened, a gentle breeze rustled through the trees, carrying with it the sounds of the jungle and the soft murmurs of conversation. Though our time in the village was nearing its end, the effects of our mission would remain long after we left. We had built more than just physical structures; we had helped to build a foundation of faith and community that would endure.

That night, as we gathered one last time under the stars, we offered prayers of thanksgiving for the journey we had taken together. We thanked God for the opportunity to serve, to learn, and to grow alongside this incredible community. And as we bid farewell to our new friends, we carried with us the knowledge that we had been part of something truly special.

As we gathered our cherished belongings and bid a heartfelt adieu to our gracious hosts, we meandered the short path to the boat dock, where our vessel awaited to whisk us back to Georgetown and the welcoming embrace of the dormitory. That night, we would find solace in Georgetown, resting before our flight to the states on the morrow.

At the dock, the warm farewells of every villager, a poignant moment that tugged at our hearts, enveloped us. Each of us embraced the villagers, including the little ones, acutely aware that this was a final parting, yet their spirits would forever linger in our memories.

We boarded the boat, savoring a serene journey up the river to Georgetown, this time unmarred by misfortune. We left behind precious memories, treasures of the heart that we would carry with us always!

In the days and weeks to come, as we returned to our own corners of the world, the memories of our time in the village would remain etched in our hearts. The lessons we had learned and the friendships we had formed would continue to inspire us, guiding us to live with purpose and compassion.

And so, with hearts full of gratitude and joy, we left the village, knowing that we had found a piece of ourselves in this remote corner of the world. We had been exactly where God wanted us to be, and for that, we were eternally grateful.

2

Why Do We Go?

The sacred missions must forever reign as the foremost priority of any church. Devotees of Jesus Christ receive their divine calling as illuminated in Matthew 28. The Great Commission urges believers to go forth and make disciples of all nations, baptizing them in the name of the Father, the Son, and the Holy Spirit. This mission is not just a task but a profound commitment to spread love, hope, and faith throughout the world. It calls for compassion, understanding, and an unwavering dedication to serve others, reaching out to those in need and offering guidance and support.

In fulfilling these sacred missions, churches become beacons of light in their communities, fostering unity and encouraging spiritual growth. Through acts of kindness, educational programs, and community services, they embody the teachings of Christ, inspiring others to live with purpose and integrity.

The journey is often challenging, requiring patience and resilience, but the impact is immeasurable. These missions transform hearts and lives, and their ripple effect extends far beyond the church walls, touching countless souls and building a legacy of faith and goodwill for generations to come.

Let's take a deeper look at that Great Commission from Matthew 28. It begins with the resurrected Jesus appearing to His disciples, offering them reassurance and authority. He declares, "All authority in heaven and on earth has been given to me." This statement emphasizes the divine power and responsibility entrusted to Him, which He then shares with His followers.

Jesus instructs His disciples to "go and make disciples of all nations." This command is both inclusive and expansive, urging them to transcend cultural and geographical boundaries to spread the message of love and salvation. It is an invitation to welcome all people into the fold, regardless of their background or status.

The directive to baptize "in the name of the Father, and of the Son, and of the Holy Spirit" underscores the Trinitarian nature of God and the unity of the divine family. Baptism serves as a sacred rite of initiation, symbolizing a commitment to the teachings of Jesus and a new life in faith.

Jesus promises His enduring presence: "And surely I am with you always, to the very end of the age." This assurance offers comfort and strength, reminding believers they are never alone in their mission. The Great Commission, therefore, is not only a call to action but also a testament to the enduring relationship between the divine and humanity, a relationship built on trust, love, and eternal companionship.

In our engagement with missions, be it through our presence or our generous contributions, we are embracing the essence of the Great Commission. Each effort, no matter how small, contributes to a larger tapestry of hope and transformation. By participating in these missions, we are not only fulfilling a divine mandate, but also enriching our own spiritual journeys. We become part of a global community that transcends borders and unites us in a common purpose: to uplift, support, and nurture one another.

These activities remind us of the power of collective action and its profound impact. Whether it's through volunteering in local outreach programs, supporting international initiatives, or simply spreading kindness in our daily interactions, each act of service resonates deeply, creating waves of positive change.

Embracing the Great Commission calls us to be mindful stewards of our resources and talents. By sharing what we have—be it time, skills, or financial support—we enable the church to extend its reach and continue its mission of love and service. This selfless giving not only strengthens the church's capacity to serve but also enriches our own lives, fostering a sense of purpose and fulfillment.

Our engagement with missions is a testament to our faith and our commitment to live out the teachings of Jesus. It is a journey of love, compassion, and unwavering dedication that transforms both the giver and the receiver, leaving a legacy of hope and unity. As we continue to embrace this calling, let us do so with open hearts and a spirit of joy, knowing that we are contributing to a world that reflects the divine love and grace of God.

Throughout the Bible, one finds many scriptures emphasizing missions, each offering unique insights into the purpose and spirit of these divine endeavors. In Acts 1:8, we find Jesus instructing His disciples with the words, "But you will receive power when the Holy Spirit comes on you; and you will be my witnesses in Jerusalem, and in all Judea and Samaria, and to the ends of the earth." This passage highlights the empowering role of the Holy Spirit in guiding believers to spread the Gospel, emphasizing both the local and global scope of their mission.

Isaiah 6:8 echoes a heartfelt response to God's call with the prophet, declaring, "Here am I. Send me!" This scripture captures the essence of willingness and readiness to serve, embodying a commitment to heed God's call and share His message of hope and redemption.

Romans 10:14-15 further underscores the necessity of missions, posing the rhetorical questions, "How, then, can they call on the one they have not believed in? And how can they believe in the one of whom they have not heard? And how can they hear without someone preaching to them?" These verses remind us of the vital role that each believer plays in spreading the good news and the importance of proclaiming God's word to all who have not yet heard it.

1 Peter 4:10 clearly emphasizes serving others with our unique gifts: "Each of you should use whatever gift you have received to serve others, as faithful stewards of God's grace in its various forms."

Together, these scriptures provide a rich tapestry of guidance and inspiration for missions, encouraging believers to embrace their calling with enthusiasm and dedication. They remind us that by working together, empowered by the Holy Spirit, and guided by faith, we can make a meaningful impact in the world, sharing God's love and transforming lives.

I have devoted a significant chapter of my life to the noble calling of mission work. Throughout my fifty-two years of ordained ministry, I have guided or participated in over sixty-eight foreign missions. I have contributed my efforts to teams across America, responding to the ravages of hurricanes and the aftermath of tornadic disasters. I share this not to dazzle you with tales of my journey, but to inspire you to partake in the essential volunteer programs the church extends to all who will heed the divine call of Christ. I would certainly never belong to a church that has no mission outreach.

In every mission, I have witnessed firsthand the transformative power of faith and service. These experiences have brought me closer to understanding the profound impact that acts of kindness and compassion can have on individuals and communities alike. Each mission has been a reminder of the resilience of the human spirit and the boundless capacity for love and healing that we all possess.

Whether rebuilding homes, providing medical care, or simply offering a listening ear, the work we do is a testament to the strength and unity found in collective action. Every moment spent in service has enriched my life immeasurably, offering insights into diverse cultures and perspectives, while reaffirming the universal truths that bind us together.

I have witnessed the restoration of hope in the eyes of those who lost everything, and I felt the gratitude of communities I helped by simply being present. These experiences have not only strengthened my faith but have also taught me the significance of humility and the importance of listening to others' stories.

As I reflect on my journey, I am reminded of the words of St. Francis of Assisi: "Preach the Gospel. When necessary, use words." This adage encapsulates the essence of mission work—living out our beliefs through tangible actions that speak volumes without uttering a single word.

I encourage you to seek opportunities to serve, to step beyond the comfort of familiar surroundings, and to embrace the joy of giving. Whether near or far, there is always a need for compassionate hearts and willing hands. By joining these efforts, you become part of a legacy of hope and transformation, contributing to a world that reflects the love and grace of God.

I distinctly remember the sensation of hand-digging a well in the enchanting land of Panama, feeling the cool earth surrounding me as I descended about twelve feet into the depths, filling buckets with soil to be hoisted to the surface by my fellow team members. It was a labor of love, each scoop of earth a testament to our shared commitment to bring the life-giving gift of water to a village in need. The sun was warm on our backs, and the air filled with the sounds of laughter and camaraderie as we worked tirelessly side by side.

The community members watched with hopeful eyes, their gratitude evident in their smiles and gestures of kindness. It was a humbling experience, one that connected us in ways words could scarcely describe. As I dug deeper, I felt profoundly connected to the land and to the people whose lives this simple, vital resource would change.

This mission was more than just a physical task; it was a spiritual journey. Each moment spent in that well reminded me of the deeper purpose behind our actions. The biblical stories of wells as places of gathering, sustenance, and divine encounters came to mind. Here, in this remote village, we were part of a modern-day parable, bringing hope and sustenance to those in need.

As the well reached completion, and the first gush of water surged forth, a cheer erupted from the gathered crowd. It was a moment of pure joy and triumph, a tangible reminder of the impact that faith in action can have. In that instant, I knew that this mission, like all the others, was a blessing—not just for those we served, but for us as well. It was a reminder of the interconnectedness of all humanity and the boundless grace we can share when we answer the call to serve.

Those who embark on mission trips are often driven by a profound love for God and a heartfelt wish to serve others. Throughout the years, countless souls have joined me on journeys to enchanting lands such as France, Spain, Puerto Rico, Jamaica, Cuba, Nicaragua, Costa Rica, and beyond. In every gaze, I have glimpsed the divine and rejoiced in their joyous spirits upon our return. Each destination has offered its own unique challenges and rewards, weaving unforgettable memories into the fabric of our shared experiences. We have built schools where learning and laughter echo through newly painted halls, planted gardens that bloom with life and nourishment, and shared stories that bridge cultures and hearts.

In France, we marveled at the blend of history and modernity, working with local communities to preserve cherished traditions while fostering innovation. In Spain, the vibrant culture and passionate spirit of the people inspired us to embrace each day with enthusiasm and open hearts. Puerto Rico's resilience in the face of adversity taught us the power of unity and determination, as we joined hands to rebuild homes and restore hope after natural disasters.

Jamaica and Cuba opened our eyes to the richness of cultural heritage and the warmth of hospitality, as we engaged in projects that supported education and sustainable development. In Nicaragua and Costa Rica, we witnessed the breathtaking beauty of nature, learning to cherish and protect the environment through conservation efforts.

These journeys are more than a series of destinations; they are pilgrimages of the soul. Each step taken, each hand held, and each smile shared has deepened our understanding of what it truly means to serve. It is a reminder that despite our differences; we are all part of the same human family, bound by love, compassion, and a shared desire to make the world a better place.

As we continue to embark on these mission trips, let us carry with us the lessons learned and the bonds formed. Let us remain inspired by the beauty of diversity and the strength found in unity. Together, we can continue to create ripples of positive change, touching lives and transforming communities, one mission at a time.

Why do I embark on these journeys? It is the irresistible call of the Great Commission given by our Lord and Savior, Jesus Christ, who compels me forward.

3

The Faces of the Children

The children of Nicaragua shine with a beauty that captivates the heart, if not in visage, then undeniably in their vibrant spirit. Their laughter echoes through the streets, a melodic testament to their resilience and joy. Each child carries a story rich with dreams and aspirations woven from the colorful tapestry of their daily lives. Despite the challenges they may face, their eyes gleam with hope and the promise of a brighter future. They play in sunlit fields and bustling neighborhoods, their energy infectious, spreading warmth to everyone around them. These young souls are not just the future of Nicaragua;

they are the heart and soul of the present, a reminder of the strength and unity that binds their communities together.

The people of Nicaragua are extremely poor. They have endured the difficulties of corrupt governments for decades, with little relief in sight. Despite these hardships, their resilience is nothing short of inspiring. Communities come together, supporting one another through thick and thin, finding strength in unity and solidarity. Families work tirelessly to provide for their loved ones, often creating small enterprises or relying on agriculture to make ends meet.

Amid adversity, they find joy in the simple things—celebrating festivals with vibrant music and dance, sharing meals that reflect the rich cultural heritage of their land, and nurturing dreams that soar beyond their immediate circumstances. Their enduring spirit is a testament to the power of hope and perseverance, proving that even in the face of adversity, the human spirit can thrive and shine brightly.

During four distinct journeys to the countryside alongside mission teams, I have beheld the struggles of the people and the shadows of poverty that envelop their lives. The people sparsely adorn their dwellings, and sustenance is a rare treasure. Yet, amidst these challenges, I have also witnessed remarkable acts of kindness and generosity. Neighbors share what little they have, and communities come together to support one another in times of need. It is in these moments that the true spirit of Nicaragua reveals itself—a spirit that is unyielding and full of compassion.

The countryside, with its lush landscapes and vibrant communities, offers a glimpse into a life deeply connected to the land and each other. Children run freely through fields, their laughter a joyful counterpoint to the struggles their families face. The elders, with wisdom etched into their faces, tell stories of resilience and hope, inspiring younger generations to dream and strive for a better tomorrow.

Throughout these journeys, I appreciate not only the beauty of Nicaragua's landscapes but also the strength and warmth of its people. Each encounter has enriched my understanding and deepened my respect for their enduring spirit. It is a reminder that even in the simplest of circumstances, there is profound dignity and an unbreakable will to persevere.

Every journey would lead us to a location ominously dubbed The Dump. Here, countless souls live within fragile cardboard shanties, foraging through the refuse to find sustenance, often days old and left untouched from a previous feast! Amidst the shadows, diseases took their toll, yet the promise of healthcare remained a distant dream. Those in the surrounding neighborhoods frequently referred to the residents of this abandoned location as "The Dump People."

I recall one visit when I rode in a pastor's jeep to bring nourishment to these resilient spirits. After sharing a warm meal, we gathered to participate in the sacred rite of Holy Communion, a moment of grace amid a harsh reality.

With a broken heart, I looked out among the dump people and saw the pain on their faces. There was no place for them to bathe, and they were completely filthy in appearance. They wore clothes they had picked from the rubbish, often ill-fitting. Smut from the constantly burning fires covered the children's faces.

After indulging and feasting upon the bountiful spread we had lovingly prepared, they settled upon the earth while I stood to share the message and offer communion.

Their attentive gazes met mine as they deciphered my halting Spanish, and in that sacred moment, the word of God became profoundly tangible. I recall tears welling in my eyes, yearning for a different place, yet I steadfastly embraced my calling as I served the bread and wine to those living in the shadows of the dump. Their warmth enveloped us, and heartfelt embraces followed our gathering. The lingering scent of their presence clings to my memory even now.

It echoes the timeless adage, "There but for the grace of God go you and I." In that poignant moment, I realized the depth of our shared humanity. Despite the stark differences in our lives, the simple act of breaking bread together bridged a gap that seemed insurmountable. The children, with their wide eyes and unyielding courage, reminded me that hope is a universal language. Their laughter, even amidst such dire circumstances, was a powerful testament to the resilience of the human spirit.

As we departed, I carried with me not just the memories of their stories and smiles, but also a renewed sense of purpose. The experience underscored the importance of compassion and empathy, of reaching out to those in need with kindness and understanding. It was a lesson in humility and a reminder of the strength that lies in community and faith.

Through the haze of smoke and the fragrance of freshly turned earth, I felt a deep connection to these people who had so graciously welcomed us into their lives. Their struggles became a call to action, urging me to continue working towards a world where everyone has access to the necessities of life and the dignity they deserve.

As we made our way back to the quaint country schoolhouse, a sanctuary for around fifty children of diverse ages, we encountered yet another tragedy. The adults prepared meals for the little ones using a stove fueled by methane gas! At the periphery of the property lay a dump pit, cloaked with a sheet of tin and featuring a tube protruding from it. They cast refuse and food remnants into the makeshift pit, which produced methane gas that rose through the tube to fuel their cooking apparatus. Though this method was fraught with peril, their inventive spirits shone through.

The children gathered around, their eyes wide with curiosity and excitement, as someone prepared lunch. Despite the precarious setup, the meals produced were nourishing and comforting, a testament to the resourcefulness of the community. They carefully prepared each dish, frequently using donated or salvaged ingredients, yet each dish possessed a rich flavor, reflecting the love and effort invested in its creation.

As we sat together in the humble schoolhouse, the children's laughter filled the air, mingling with the tantalizing aromas wafting from the kitchen. Their cheerful chatter spoke of dreams and aspirations, of adventures and friendships, painting a picture of hope and possibility.

The teachers, dedicated and passionate, worked tirelessly to provide not just education but also a nurturing environment where these young minds could flourish. They understood that beyond academic lessons, instilling a sense of self-worth and resilience was equally vital. With limited resources, they crafted lessons that were as imaginative as they were instructive, fostering a love for learning that transcended the confines of their circumstances.

In this small haven, the children learned not only the basics of reading and writing but also the values of kindness, cooperation, and perseverance. Their teachers instilled dreams in them that transcended their current realities, helping them envision a future where they could fully realize their potential.

Leaving the schoolhouse, I felt a profound sense of admiration for the people who, despite overwhelming challenges, continued to invest in the future of their children. Their unwavering belief in the power of education and community was a beacon of hope, illuminating a path toward a brighter tomorrow.

This experience reaffirmed my commitment to supporting such initiatives and to working alongside these resilient communities in their pursuit of a better life. It reminded me that every minor act of kindness, every effort to uplift those in need, contributes to a world where every child can dream, thrive, and shine.

In the end, this journey was not just about providing aid; it was about building bridges of love and solidarity. It was about recognizing the beauty in every soul and the potential for change that lives within us all.

4

Ecuador's Guinea Pig Feast

We were embarking on a heartfelt journey to Ecuador as a united team, destined to empower women with the enchanting skill of crafting ovens from humble cardboard boxes—an art one of our members had mastered at mission school the previous year. Together, we would partner with the local church to build new facilities for their school and illuminate each day with the joys of Vacation Bible School.

Our days were filled with laughter, creativity, and a shared sense of purpose as we embraced the vibrant culture and warm hospitality of the Ecuadorian community. The air buzzed with excitement as we gathered materials for the ovens, transforming simple cardboard into a tool of empowerment and sustainability. We had carried rolls of aluminum foil with us to surround the cardboard for the ovens, and the local women were taught how to construct them.

Each evening, as the sun dipped below the horizon, painting the sky in hues of orange and pink, we reflected on the day's accomplishments and the bonds we were forging. The locals welcomed us with open arms, eager to learn and teach in return, sharing their traditions and stories that deepened our understanding of their rich heritage.

The Vacation Bible School sessions became a highlight, as children's laughter echoed through the halls, their eyes wide with wonder and curiosity. Through songs, stories, and games, we sparked their imaginations and nurtured their spirits, creating memories that would linger long after our journey had ended. In our fragmented Spanish, accompanied by our faithful interpreters, we exchanged the sacred words of Christ, united in prayer, and worshipped as one harmonious family.

As our time in Ecuador unfolded, it became clear that this journey was not just about what we could give, but also what we could receive. We were learning invaluable lessons of resilience, community, and the power of working together towards a common goal.

On our final evening with the community, they graciously hosted a dinner at the church, a heartfelt gesture of gratitude for the gifts we had shared. As the table was adorned, substantial aluminum pans emerged, each cradling a baked creature within. Curiosity piqued. I inquired with a church member about the dish, and she revealed it was guinea pig, a cherished staple in Ecuador. These creatures roam freely in the fields and woods, growing much larger than the adorable little companions found in homes across the states.

As our team discovered the peculiar type of meat laid before us, I gently reminded them to express gratitude for the warm hospitality of our hosts. With a hint of reluctance, they began to partake in the delicacy of guinea pig. A leg was presented to me, and though I struggled to summon the courage to savor it, I pressed on, each bite accompanied by the refreshing juice served alongside.

The taste was unique, a blend of unfamiliar flavors and textures that marked this moment as a true cultural exchange. As we shared this meal, laughter and conversation flowed around the table, bridging the gap between our worlds and deepening our connection with our Ecuadorian friends.

Our hosts watched our reactions with amusement and pride, recounting tales of how guinea pigs had been a part of their traditions for generations. It was more than just a meal; it was a symbol of their heritage and an invitation to understand and appreciate their way of life.

As the evening wore on, stories and smiles were shared, fostering a sense of unity and mutual respect. We learned that in embracing the unfamiliar, we gained a richer understanding and a profound appreciation for the diversity of the world. This shared experience reminded us that true connection often lies in stepping beyond our comfort zones and opening our hearts to new experiences.

As we prepared to leave Ecuador, we carried with us not only the memories of our projects and the friendships we had formed but also a deeper appreciation for the beautiful tapestry of cultures that make up our world. Our journey had been transformative, leaving an indelible mark on our hearts and a renewed commitment to fostering understanding and kindness wherever our paths might lead.

Guinea Pig, anyone?

5

Something Greater than Ourselves

While we traverse the intriguing realm of missions, allow me to unveil three profound quotes that have graced my path on this wondrous journey of life.

In the cinematic gem "The Way," Martin Sheen, a businessman ensnared in the whirlwind of his daily grind, receives a poignant message from his son, who is embarking on an adventurous quest... The quote that resonates deeply is, "You don't choose a life, Dad. You live one." This simple yet profound statement serves as a powerful reminder to embrace the present moment and cherish the experiences that life offers, rather than being consumed by the relentless pursuit of success or material gains.

Another quote that has profoundly affected my perspective is from the timeless novel "The Alchemist" by Paulo Coelho: "When you want something, all the universe conspires to help you achieve it." This quote inspires courage and hope, encouraging us to pursue our dreams with unwavering determination, knowing that the forces of the universe align to support our aspirations.

I also find solace in the words of Maya Angelou: "We may encounter many defeats, but we must not be defeated." Her wisdom reminds us of the resilience of the human spirit, urging us to rise above challenges and continue our journey with grace and strength. Never say that you can't do something! You never know until you've tried. I never once thought I'd be getting on an airplane and flying for several hours to reach a destination for a mission, but I did. And now I've done it on many such occasions, venturing into the unknown to share my life and ministry with others whom I've never met.

These quotes, each a beacon of wisdom, guide us along the path of life, illuminating the way with insights that enrich our existence and inspire us to live fully, with purpose and passion. In moments of uncertainty or doubt, they serve as gentle reminders we are not alone on this journey. They encourage us to seek new horizons, to embrace the unknown with open hearts, and to remain steadfast in the face of adversity.

As we navigate the complexities of our individual paths, these words of wisdom become companions, offering solace and motivation. They teach us to see beyond the surface, to find meaning in every experience, and to appreciate the unique tapestry of moments that define our lives. Let these quotes be the sparks that ignite our inner fire, propelling us forward with courage and conviction as we continue to explore the vast landscape of life's possibilities.

Another cherished gem of wisdom comes from the illustrious Pablo Casals, who proclaimed, "The capacity to care is the thing that gives life its deepest meaning and significance." This profound insight reminds us of the importance of compassion and empathy in our lives. Caring for others not only enriches our own lives but also creates a ripple effect of kindness and connection that can transform the world. In a time when the pace of life can often lead us to overlook the needs of those around us, Casals' words serve as a gentle nudge to pause, to listen, and to extend a helping hand where we can.

By embracing the act of caring, we cultivate a sense of community and belonging, fostering relationships that nurture our souls and bring joy to our hearts. It is through these connections that we find true fulfillment and purpose, realizing that the greatest achievements are those that touch the lives of others in meaningful ways. As we carry forward the wisdom of these quotes, let us strive to live with open hearts, always ready to care for and share in the journey of life with those we encounter along the way.

Billy Dee Williams once said, "Sometimes you get lucky and become part of something bigger than yourself." This sentiment beautifully captures the essence of serendipity and the magic that unfolds when we open ourselves to the unexpected opportunities life offers. It reminds us that while we may chart our own paths, there are moments when the universe intervenes, guiding us toward experiences that expand our horizons and connect us to a greater purpose.

Being part of something larger than ourselves can be life-changing, allowing us to contribute to causes that uplift others and make a lasting impact. It encourages us to step outside our comfort zones, embrace collaboration, and discover the profound joy of being woven into the fabric of a collective journey.

In those moments of connection, we find a deeper sense of belonging and fulfillment, realizing that our individual actions can resonate far beyond our own lives. Let us cherish these opportunities, for they not only enrich our own experiences but also strengthen the bonds that unite us with others, crafting a tapestry of shared dreams and endeavors.

As we continue to navigate our personal journeys, let Williams' words remind us to remain open to the serendipitous gifts life presents. Embrace the chance to be part of something greater and let your unique contributions add to the mosaic of collective human experience, enriching the world in ways you may never have imagined.

At the heartfelt urging of my cherished friend, Dr. Frank Terry, I embarked on my inaugural mission trip. He was insistent, refusing to accept "no" as a response. My role was to be the melodious spirit of the journey, strumming my guitar as we ventured to the sultry realms along the Costa Rica/Panama border.

For a fortnight, I attempted to deter his fervent enthusiasm, but before I could gather my thoughts, he had reached out to my church, where I served as pastor, requesting they conjure the $800 needed for my passage. Much to my surprise, the following Sunday, the steward of our congregation stood before us in the pulpit, heralding the news of their generous support! That was the first moment I learned of their willingness to send me forth. How could I refuse to go?

It was the start of something beautiful and life-changing for me. Brother Frank knew I was young and energetic and would make a great candidate for future mission trips and would even become the team leader of most of them. From that humble beginning, I have served as president and vice president of our conference VOLUNTEERS IN MISSIONS committee and as vice president of our Conference Board of Missions. These roles have provided me with invaluable experiences and have allowed me to witness the transformative power of service in action. Each mission trip has been a unique opportunity to connect with diverse communities, learn from distinct cultures, and contribute to meaningful projects that uplift those in need.

Through these journeys, I have discovered the true essence of leadership—it's not just about guiding others, but also about listening, learning, and growing together. The friendships and bonds formed during these missions have enriched my life beyond measure and have taught me the importance of humility and gratitude.

These experiences have deepened my understanding of global interconnectedness and the shared responsibility we must support one another. I am continually inspired by the resilience and kindness of the people I have met, and their stories fuel my passion to continue this rewarding work.

Looking back, I feel immense gratitude for Brother Frank's gentle push, which set me on this path of service and discovery. As I continue to lead and take part in missions, I am committed to fostering an environment where compassion and collaboration thrive, ensuring that every project brings hope and positive change to the communities we serve.

I am also deeply aware of the profound impact these missions have on my life. Each journey is a reminder of the beauty and diversity of the human spirit and the limitless potential. We all must make a difference. The stories we share, the challenges we overcome, and the friendships we forge are testaments to the transformative power of collective action and empathy.

As I reflect on these experiences, I am filled with a sense of purpose and a desire to continue this journey with an open heart. The lessons I've learned from those I've met along the way have left an indelible mark on my soul, teaching me the true meaning of resilience, hope, and the importance of giving back.

In the years to come, I hope to inspire others to embark on their own missions of service, to embrace the unexpected, and to discover the joy of being part of something greater than themselves. Together, we can create a world where compassion knows no boundaries and where every individual can thrive.

Let us continue to build bridges of understanding and love, and let our shared mission be a beacon of light in a world that sometimes feels divided. With each step we take, may we bring a little more kindness into the world, leaving a legacy of hope and unity for generations to come.

6

Missions at Home

Missions can unfold in the most unexpected places. Recently, my wife attended a gathering for ladies, where the speaker was none other than the manager of our local food bank. She illuminated the church ladies on the breadth of their compassionate outreach, providing sustenance to approximately 1,000 individuals each month. This noble endeavor typically involves giving a box filled with canned goods, staples, and other essentials to each family. With heartfelt urgency, she emphasized the pressing need for both food and financial contributions. Our community's extensive assistance also surprised Renee, supplying many families with essentials each month.

Inspired by this revelation, Renee felt a deep calling to contribute more actively. She discussed her thoughts with me, and we both agreed that we could do more to support this vital cause. We could add the Food Bank to our list of causes for a monthly contribution.

We visited the food bank together to learn more about their operations and see firsthand the impact of their work. As we walked through the bustling center, volunteers sorting donations and packing boxes warmly greeted us with care. A sense of purpose and community spirit pervaded the atmosphere.

The manager, whom Renee had met at the gathering, took the time to show us around. She explained how each donation, no matter how small, contributes to making a significant difference in the lives of those they help. The stories of families who found relief moved us and gave us hope through the food bank's efforts.

As we left the food bank that day, our hearts were full of gratitude for the opportunity to be involved in such a worthy cause. We knew that our efforts, combined with the generosity of others, could help lighten the burden for many in our community.

In the bustling heart of a great city, during my days of shepherding a church, I embarked on a heartfelt ministry to three nursing homes each week. Accompanied by several devoted ladies from my congregation, we filled the air with melodies, singing cherished songs alongside the residents. Each visit culminated in a touching devotion and a moment of prayer before we took our leave. Though our time together was but thirty fleeting minutes, the warmth of gratitude from those dear souls enveloped us, a testament to the profound impact of our humble gestures.

The connections we formed during those visits were truly special, transcending the boundaries of age and circumstance. Each resident had their own story, a tapestry woven with experiences and wisdom that they graciously shared with us. In return, we offered our companionship and a listening ear, creating a bridge between generations.

Over time, our small group became a regular fixture, eagerly expected by the residents and staff alike. We learned their favorite hymns and crafted our devotions to resonate with their hearts, ensuring each session was meaningful and joyful.

The experience taught us the power of presence—the simple act of being there, offering kindness and understanding. It reminded us that, no matter how busy life becomes, taking the time to connect with others can bring immeasurable joy and fulfillment, both to those we visit and to ourselves.

Even after I moved to another church in another city, those church ladies continued the weekly ministry to those three nursing homes. I was deeply touched because of their devotion to a mission they had undertaken now on their own.

As I reflect on those days, I am filled with a sense of gratitude for the opportunity to serve and for the lessons learned from those wise and gentle souls. They, in their quiet strength, have left an indelible mark on my heart, and I carry their stories with me always.

Missions may unfold in any corner of the world, be it amidst the vibrant pulse of the inner city or the serene embrace of the countryside. From the bustling streets of urban centers to the tranquil lanes of rural communities, each mission carries with it the potential to transform lives and foster connections. Often, it is in the least expected places we find our purpose and the chance to make a meaningful impact.

In these diverse settings, individuals come together, united by a shared desire to uplift and support one another. Whether it's volunteering at a local shelter, organizing community events, or simply offering a listening ear to someone in need, every act of kindness contributes to a greater good.

As we navigate through life's journey, it's important to remain open to these opportunities for service and connection. They enrich our experiences, broaden our perspectives, and remind us of the inherent goodness that exists within us all. By embracing these missions, we not only help others but also discover new layers of compassion and empathy within ourselves.

In doing so, we build a tapestry of community that is stronger, more resilient, and filled with hope for a brighter future. We go beyond ourselves to what we can do together.

Here are a few noble missions within your community that you might embrace:

Disaster Relief: Providing shelter, nourishment, or supplies in times of crisis.

Literacy Programs: Guiding adults or children in the art of reading and writing.

Food Assistance: operating food pantries or organizing meal services for the hungry.

Environmental Projects: revitalizing parks, planting verdant trees, or starting recycling drives.

Support for Seniors: visiting nursing homes or lending a hand with errands.

Youth Outreach: mentoring, tutoring, or organizing spirited sports activities.

Health Initiatives: Hosting complimentary health check-ups or invigorating fitness classes.

Clothing Drives: gathering and distributing garments to those in need.

Community Beautification: Adorning walls with murals, cleaning the streets, or tending to gardens.

Support for Emergency Responders: Preparing meals or hosting appreciation events for local heroes—police, firefighters, and EMTs.

Each of these missions offers a unique opportunity to make a meaningful impact on the lives of others and strengthen the bonds within your community. By participating in these initiatives, you not only contribute to the well-being of those around you but also find fulfillment and a sense of purpose.

As you consider these options, think about what resonates most with you and where your skills and passions align. Whether you have an affinity for organization, a passion for teaching, or a love for the outdoors, there's a mission that can benefit from your talents.

Engaging in community service is a powerful way to connect with others, learn from diverse perspectives, and cultivate a spirit of empathy and generosity. It reminds us we are all part of a larger tapestry, each thread contributing to the beauty and strength of the whole.

So, take that first step. Reach out to local organizations, gather a group of friends or family members, and explore the possibilities. Together, you can create a ripple effect of positive change, leaving an impression on your community and beyond.

People in some of my churches often complained about their pastor taking off on a mission trip once a year. They often said things like, "There's enough mission work to do right here at home!"" And my comeback to them is, "Then do those missions. No excuse!"

Pay it forward!

7

Our Venezuela Encounter

As the aircraft gracefully veered to the left, it began its descent into the vibrant city of Caracas, Venezuela, unveiling the picturesque mountain town perched at the northernmost edge of South America. A flutter of anxiety danced within me as the plane quaked and trembled, confronting the warm embrace of land meeting sea. Yet, my fellow travelers brimmed with excitement, ready to embark on their inaugural mission in this foreign land.

Upon our arrival, the local pastor gave us a warm welcome and assisted us in loading our gear and luggage into two waiting trucks. Soon, we ventured deep into the heart of the country, near the meandering Apure River. There, nestled in a small, impoverished village, lay our purpose: to construct a humble church within a fortnight. Though it would not be grand, it would stand as a beacon of hope, complete with handcrafted pews, a simple pulpit, and unadorned windows.

The villagers greeted us with palpable enthusiasm, eager to welcome our team. They paired us off and assigned us to our new homes for the next two weeks. My friend and fellow missioner found solace in a modest home, where we would rest upon single beds filled with straw, embracing the simplicity of our surroundings.

The scent of freshly turned earth and the soft hum of insects filled the air, creating an atmosphere that felt both foreign and strangely familiar. As we settled into our routine, the villagers showed an eagerness to help, their hands and hearts open to the task ahead. Every morning, the sun rose over the lush landscape, casting a golden hue on the day's labor.

Children, with bright eyes and curious smiles, often gathered around, their laughter a joyous soundtrack to our work. They marveled at the tools we used, sometimes mimicking our actions with sticks and stones. It was in these moments of shared joy and purpose that the true spirit of community shone through, bridging any cultural or language barriers.

As the days passed, the church took shape, its walls rising steadily against the backdrop of the verdant hills. Each nail, each piece of wood, was more than just construction material; it was a testament to the collective effort and hope for a brighter future. The villagers expressed their gratitude through gestures of kindness—shared meals, exchanged stories, and forged friendships under the sweltering sun.

In the evenings, we gathered with our hosts, sharing stories of our homes and dreams. The bonds we formed were as strong as the foundations we laid, promising to endure beyond our brief time there. With each passing day, I felt a deepening connection to this land and its people—a reminder of the shared humanity that unites us all, regardless of the miles that separate our worlds.

With an additional day of grace, our pastor missionary beckoned us to embark on an adventure to encounter a native tribe of Christians nestled along the Apure River, near the enchanting Amazon. We gathered on the riverbank, anticipation swirling in the air as we awaited our vessels to glide downstream and whisk us away.

Before long, four dugout canoes emerged, helmed by skilled tribesmen. We settled four team members into each vessel, and with a flourish, the canoes turned and began their ascent against the gentle current. Our pastor friend cautioned us against dipping our hands into the water, for it harbored the fearsome piranha, invoking a reverent trepidation within our hearts. With the canoes hovering merely six inches above the surface, the warning resonated deeply.

After a spell of rowing that felt like an eternity, we reached the village, a tapestry of thatched huts adorned with the simplicity of life and a quaint brush-arbor standing as a testament to their faith.

The villagers emerged from their homes, their faces alight with warmth and curiosity. They greeted us with open arms and songs of welcome, their voices harmonizing with the symphony of the jungle. It was a moment of profound connection, where language barriers dissolved, and the shared rhythm of life united us all.

As we settled into the village, we marveled at the ingenuity and resilience of the community. The brush-arbor, though humble, was a sacred space where the villagers gathered to worship and find solace. It stood as a symbol of their unwavering faith and the strength that bound them together.

Our hosts eagerly shared stories of their ancestors, tales woven with the wisdom of the land and the rivers that sustained them. We shared our own stories, finding common threads of hope and dreams that transcended cultures. The exchange was enriching, a reminder of the beauty found in diversity and the unspoken bonds that tie us all.

In the afternoon, we joined the villagers in a communal feast, where laughter and camaraderie flowed as freely as the river beside us. We caught piranha from the river that was used for our lunch, prepared with love and care by the natives, which was a testament to their generosity and the spirit of the community that defined their lives.

In those cherished moments, beneath the sprawling tapestry of the Amazon sky, we came to understand that we were not mere visitors but threads woven into a grander family, bound by faith, hope, and the shared odyssey of existence. After a time of communion under the verdant arbor, we departed that hallowed ground in our canoes, gently guided back to our chariots, embarking on the journey home for our last night.

As dawn painted the horizon, we found ourselves at the airport by 5 am, eagerly expecting a 6 am voyage back to the bustling Miami airport, where a connecting flight awaited us to Tallahassee. Gazing down upon the expansive embrace of Venezuela through the airplane's porthole, we held in our hearts the indelible memories of a journey that transcended mere geographical exploration. The faces of the villagers, their laughter, and the gentle wisdom shared during our brief sojourn lingered in our minds like cherished snapshots of a dream. Each moment spent in that vibrant land had etched a profound sense of connection and purpose within us.

As the plane soared higher, the landscape below faded into a patchwork of greens and browns, yet the impact of our mission remained vividly alive. We had arrived intending to build and offer hope, but in truth, we had received so much more than we gave. The resilience and warmth of the people had taught us invaluable lessons about strength, simplicity, and the universal language of kindness.

Reflecting on our time in Venezuela, we realized we forged bonds that were not confined to the physical structures we constructed or the communal meals we shared. Instead, these bonds became woven into the very fabric of our being, a testament to the power of human connection and the enduring spirit of community.

As we touched down in Miami, the hustle and bustle of the airport stood in stark contrast to the serene simplicity we had left behind. Yet, the sense of unity and understanding we carried with us was a gentle reminder of the journey's true purpose. It was a reminder that, no matter where our paths may lead, the experiences and friendships formed in that distant land would forever illuminate our lives, guiding us toward a brighter future.

8

Katrina's Mission

After eight hours in our church van, having departed from Sylvania, Georgia, we were eager to arrive at our destination. The journey revealed the haunting aftermath of Hurricane Katrina, etched into small towns, barren stretches of interstate, and the coastline of Mississippi. An unsettling silence enveloped the highway and the towns we passed, with few vehicles gracing the roads. Blue tarps adorned many rooftops, a poignant testament to the storm's enduring scars.

As we drove further, the remnants of the hurricane's fury became even more palpable. We could see trees uprooted and fields that once flourished now lying desolate.

Despite the devastation, there was a sense of resilience in the air. Working together, locals slowly rebuilt their communities, restoring what the hurricane had destroyed.

And so, we drew near to the shimmering expanse of Lake Pontchartrain, where the dam had succumbed to nature's fury, unleashing a deluge upon the land merely two weeks prior, in the wake of Katrina's wrath. With trepidation, I guided our van across the vast waters, navigating the floating pontoon sections that danced upon the surface. It was undeniably a heart-pounding moment as we cautiously journeyed to the other side, crossing the threshold into Louisiana. I could only think of having to come back over the temporary bridge on our return home!

As we traversed the shimmering expanse of the lake, a vast wilderness unfurled before our eyes, revealing the haunting aftermath of devastation that marked the outskirts of New Orleans, our awaited destination. Scattered along the highways were rescue vehicles and trucks brimming with supplies—an offering of food and water from kind-hearted volunteers who had journeyed to this beleaguered city from distant lands like Ogden, Utah, Dearborn, Michigan, and Sylvania, Georgia. Each home bore the telltale sign of struggle, adorned with blue tarps that fluttered gently in the breeze. A sea of azure blanketed the downtown area as our van inched across the bridge near the Superdome, a once-bustling sanctuary where thousands had gathered mere days prior, awaiting buses that would whisk them away to safety. Now, the dome stood silent, a ghost of its former self, mirroring the stillness of the surrounding city.

Radiant smiles and welcoming embraces greeted us upon our arrival in the vibrant heart of New Orleans. Hope blossomed here, even amidst the remnants of hardship. Volunteers from diverse paths of life gathered, bound by a noble mission to restore and mend. The spirit of unity was palpable, and as we established our home base within the walls of a local United Methodist Church, an immense gratitude enveloped us for being woven into this shared tapestry of resilience. For the week, we would nestle in sleeping bags upon the floors of Sunday School rooms, preparing our meals in the church's bustling kitchen—the sanctuary stood as one of the few havens in the area blessed with a generator.

In the evenings, after a day filled with demanding work and heartfelt conversations, we found solace in the church's community hall. Here, we gathered to share meals and stories, laughter echoing through the room as we counted the day's events. Each person brought a unique perspective, adding richness to the experience and fostering connections that transcended backgrounds.

Despite the challenges, there was a certain magic in the air. Music, an intrinsic part of New Orleans' soul, drifted through the streets—an uplifting reminder of the city's indomitable spirit. Local musicians, undeterred by the chaos of recent weeks, serenaded us with melodies that soothed weary hearts, their tunes weaving through the night like a gentle balm.

One night, our team ventured downtown and strolled down the streets to witness the damage. Crowds of people clamored through the wreckage. At one point, I bumped into a young, white-haired individual that my team would later tell me was Anderson Cooper of CNN. I did not know who Anderson Cooper was but later learned that he was there covering the storm and its aftermath.

It was hot—brutally hot. We donned white FEMA jumpsuits and masks every day before entering homes to clean up the mess and strip the walls. We could only stand to stay in a house for fifteen minutes at the time and would soak wet from sweat. It would be this way each day during our stay.

As the days unfolded, our efforts bore fruit. Houses slowly transformed from shells of desolation to homes brimming with life once more. The gratitude expressed by the residents was humbling; their optimism and determination inspired us to push through our own fatigue. It was a testament to the power of community and the profound impact of collective action.

Our experience in New Orleans was more than just a relief effort; it was a journey of understanding and empathy. We learned that in the face of adversity, humanity's greatest strength lies in its ability to come together, to lift one another up, and to find hope amidst the rubble. As our time in the city ended, we carried with us not only memories of hard work and camaraderie but also a renewed belief in the resilience of the human spirit.

In the days that followed, we worked side by side with the residents, clearing debris, repairing homes, and listening to their stories. Each narrative was a testament to human strength and perseverance. And though the road to recovery was long, the bonds we formed with the people we met served as a reminder that even in the darkest times, kindness and community light the way forward.

As we journeyed back home, I once more traversed the shimmering expanse of Lake Pontchartrain, yet this time, fear held no sway over me. Fatigued and worn, our hearts yearned for the embrace of Sylvania. Yet, the memories of our adventures, the sights we beheld, and the experiences we cherished in the vibrant tapestry of New Orleans would forever etch their magic upon our souls!

We drove onward, the rhythm of the road soothing our tired minds, each mile bringing us closer to the familiar comforts of home. The journey profoundly affected each of us, as evidenced by the muted chatter and shared reflections filling the van. We spoke of the resilience we had witnessed, the warmth of the people who welcomed us, and the unwavering spirit of a city that refused to be defeated.

As we crossed state lines, the landscape gradually transformed from the coastal remnants of the storm to the gentle rolling fields of Georgia. The familiar sights and sounds of home beckoned, yet there was a newfound appreciation for the strength and unity we had been a part of.

Back in Sylvania, life resumed its usual pace, but each of us carried a piece of New Orleans with us—a reminder of the power of community and the importance of reaching out to those in need. We continued to draw inspiration from this journey, letting its lessons shape our actions and perspectives long after we unpacked the van and shared our stories.

With hearts full of gratitude and spirits renewed, we returned to our daily lives, forever changed by the kindness and resilience we had encountered. The experience had not only enriched our understanding of the world but also deepened our connection to one another, weaving a tapestry of compassion and hope that would endure through time.

I would return twice again to help the people of New Orleans recover from the hurricane. Each trip filled me with hope as I witnessed groups from across America helping those precious people. We need each other in situations like this. Why not offer your services today to those who are in need?

9

The Missionary Named Paul

St. Paul's missionary journeys illuminate the remarkable transformative power of faith and an unwavering devotion to the Great Commission. Paul, a pivotal apostle in the early days of Christianity, undertook journeys that transcended the merely physical. His odysseys spanned expansive lands, uniting diverse cultures, and languages, while his steadfast commitment to disseminating the Gospel stands as a timeless beacon for missionaries across the ages.

Paul's journeys took him through regions such as Asia Minor, Greece, and Rome, where he courageously spread the teachings of Christ despite facing numerous obstacles.

His ability to connect with people from various backgrounds showed a deep understanding of cultural sensitivities and an extraordinary capacity for empathy. Through his letters, Paul addressed the nascent Christian communities, offering guidance and encouragement, which continue to resonate with believers today.

His epistles, filled with theological insights and practical advice, not only strengthened the early Church but also laid a foundation for Christian doctrine. Paul's encounters with opposition from both secular authorities and religious leaders highlighted his resilience and unwavering faith. He navigated these challenges with a grace that inspired many to follow Christ, embodying the essence of a true servant leader.

Paul's personal transformation—from a persecutor of Christians to a devoted apostle—serves as a powerful testament to the redemptive potential of faith. His life story underscores the message that no one is beyond the reach of God's grace, and it encourages individuals to embrace change and pursue a path of righteousness.

St. Paul's enduring legacy reminds us of his mission's impact and how his teachings continue to shape and inspire the spiritual journeys of countless people worldwide.

This discourse embarks on a profound exploration of the spiritual essence woven throughout Paul's missionary journeys, highlighting the theological richness of his message, the unwavering resilience he displayed in the face of suffering, and the ultimate sacrifice he rendered for the cause of Christ. Through the lens of his church establishments, his letters brimming with encouragement and guidance, and his encounters with formidable opposition, we reveal the very heart of his mission: to share the message of salvation with all. This study explores the significant challenges Paul faced—imprisonment, beatings, and martyrdom—highlighting the genuine cost of discipleship and the unwavering faith that sustained him through life's tumultuous storms.

With each hardship, Paul refined and strengthened his faith. His ability to remain steadfast amidst adversity exemplifies the fortitude required to advance the Gospel in challenging environments. Paul's theological insights continue to offer a profound understanding of grace, redemption, and the transformative power of faith.

In examining the legacy of St. Paul, we also find a blueprint for building resilient communities of faith. His emphasis on unity, love, and service within the early

Church underscores the importance of fostering relationships grounded in Christ's teachings. By nurturing these principles, modern believers can create inclusive and thriving communities that reflect the early Church's spirit of togetherness and mission.

St. Paul's life and teachings serve as a timeless reminder of the power of conviction and the sacrifices required to bring light to the world. His story encourages us to embrace our own spiritual journeys with courage and dedication, ever mindful of the enduring legacy that one life, fully committed to a divine calling, can leave upon the world.

Through the journey of St. Paul's life and ministry, contemporary missionaries can glean profound lessons on weaving the Gospel into diverse contexts, navigating hardships with unwavering grace, and nurturing enduring communities of faith, ensuring that his legacy continues to illuminate and guide the path ahead.

His remarkable journey serves as a testament to the transformative power of faith and the profound impact one individual can have on the world. As modern missionaries embark on their own paths, they can draw inspiration from St. Paul's tireless dedication and his ability to adapt the message of hope and love to resonate with varied cultures and societies. His example encourages a spirit of inclusivity, reminding us that the message of Christ transcends cultural and linguistic barriers, fostering unity among believers.

Besides his adaptability, St. Paul's resilience in the face of adversity teaches the importance of steadfastness and perseverance. Despite facing imprisonment, persecution, and martyrdom, he remained committed to his mission, driven by an unshakable faith. This resilience is a powerful reminder for those who encounter challenges in their own spiritual journeys, underscoring the importance of maintaining hope and courage in the face of trials.

St. Paul's writings continue to provide valuable theological insights that enrich our understanding of Christian doctrine. His teachings on grace, redemption, and the nature of the Church offer timeless wisdom that guides believers in their spiritual growth and communal life. By studying his letters, modern Christians can deepen their faith and draw closer to the divine.

St. Paul's life and mission offer a blueprint for living a life of purpose and impact anchored in faith and love. His legacy challenges us to engage with the world actively, embodying the teachings of Christ in our actions and relationships. As we strive to make a positive difference, we remember that, like St. Paul's, our lives can testify to faith's enduring power to transform hearts and communities.

Fantastic! Let's build the body of your discourse by dividing it into key sections with detailed points. I'll outline each section, ensuring we stay focused on the spiritual significance, his sufferings, and his ultimate sacrifice.

The Missionary Spirit of St. Paul

Responding to the Divine Summons: Paul's metamorphosis upon the road to Damascus (Acts 9) heralded the dawn of his fervent missionary spirit. Transitioning from a fierce adversary of Christians to a devoted apostle, his conversion beautifully illustrates the profound ability of God to transform hearts with radical grace.

This pivotal moment not only marked the beginning of Paul's mission but also serves as a powerful narrative of redemption and purpose. His dramatic encounter with the divine light on the way to Damascus encapsulates the core message of hope and renewal that lies at the heart of the Christian faith. From that day forward, Paul became an ardent advocate for the Gospel, embodying the transformative power of encountering Christ.

His newfound zeal propelled him to spread the message of salvation everywhere, fueled by an unwavering commitment to his divine calling. This transformation testifies to faith's boundless possibilities and the miraculous redirection of lives toward a higher purpose. It also highlights the importance of remaining open to change and embracing the journey of faith with humility and courage.

Paul's story inspires believers to trust in personal transformation, showing that God's grace can redeem even the most blemished past. His life is a beacon of hope for those who seek a fresh start, illustrating that every individual has the potential to become a vessel of light and love in the world. Reflecting on Paul's conversion and subsequent mission inspires us to embark on our own paths with the same fervor and dedication, confident in the transformative power of a life surrendered to divine will.

In the vibrant tapestry of the Great Commission, Paul personified the divine mandate found in Matthew 28:19, urging the creation of disciples across all nations. His travels mirrored a steadfast devotion to heralding the Gospel to both Jews and Gentiles alike.

With an unwavering commitment to this sacred mission, Paul traversed diverse landscapes, each journey a testament to his dedication and faith. His missionary zeal was not just about geographical expansion, but about reaching the hearts and souls of individuals from all levels of society, breaking down barriers, and fostering a sense of unity under the banner of Christ's love.

An incredible adaptability and a deep respect for the cultures he encountered characterized Paul's approach. He effectively communicated the timeless truths of the Gospel in ways that resonated with varied audiences, whether through philosophical discourse in Athens or through personal testimonies in intimate gatherings. His ability to contextualize the message of Christ without compromising its essence remains a guiding example for missionaries today.

Beyond his physical travels, Paul's epistles served as an extension of his missionary work, bridging distances, and connecting communities with messages of hope, correction, and encouragement. These letters, rich with theological insight and practical wisdom, laid a foundational framework for the burgeoning Christian Church, ensuring that the seeds he planted would continue to flourish long after his departure.

Paul's life and ministry exemplify a profound commitment to living out the Great Commission, inspiring generations of believers to share the transformative power of the Gospel with courage and compassion. His legacy is a call to action for all who seek to bring light to the world, reminding us that with faith and perseverance, we too can make a lasting impact.

Paul's life reminds missionaries of the power of surrendering fully to God's call. With unwavering faith and dedication, he embodied the essence of living a life led by divine purpose. His journey illustrates that true fulfillment comes from aligning one's heart with God's will, allowing His grace to guide every step. Today's missionaries, reflecting on Paul's legacy, embrace their own callings with open hearts, bravely and hopefully facing challenges.

Paul's story is a testament to the transformative power of faith, urging believers to trust in God's plan and to remain steadfast, even when the path is fraught with obstacles. His willingness to endure suffering for the sake of the Gospel serves as a powerful reminder that sacrifice and hardship are integral parts of a life devoted to Christ. By following his example, missionaries can find strength in their mission, knowing that their efforts contribute to a greater purpose and have the potential to touch countless lives.

Paul's teachings emphasize the importance of community and fellowship, reminding us we are never alone in our spiritual quests. By fostering unity and love within the Church, missionaries can create supportive environments where faith can flourish and grow. This spirit of togetherness, inspired by Paul's letters and actions, continues to resonate across generations, encouraging believers to work together in spreading the message of hope and redemption.

Paul's life and teachings offer a blueprint for living with intention and impact, challenging modern missionaries to pursue their vocations with passion and unwavering faith. His legacy is a beacon of light, guiding us on our own journeys and inspiring us to leave a lasting mark on the world through our commitment to God's call.

10

Modern Echoes of Paul's Journeys

The fervent missionary spirit that ignited the heart of St. Paul echoed through the ages, reverberating in the remarkable journey of Adoniram Judson, a trailblazer among missionaries to Burma in the 19th century. Mirroring Paul's own odyssey, Judson faced formidable trials and profound sacrifices while spending time in a Burmese prison. Yet it was his steadfast faith in the life-altering essence of the gospel that guided him through every tempest.

His unwavering commitment to spreading the message of Christ led him to navigate the uncharted waters of cultural immersion, where understanding and empathy became his compass. Judson's ability to adapt and learn the Burmese language was not just a testament to his intellectual prowess but also a reflection of his deep respect for the people he was called to serve.

In the face of adversity, Judson's resilience shone brightly. He approached every challenge with prayerful determination, seeing each obstacle as a chance to strengthen his reliance on divine providence. His work laid the groundwork for future generations of missionaries, inspiring them to embrace the transformative power of faith and to carry forward the mission of love and compassion.

Judson's legacy is a poignant reminder that the seeds of faith, once sown with love and perseverance, can blossom into a vibrant testimony of hope and redemption. Just as Paul's teachings continue to inspire believers worldwide, Judson's contributions to the Christian mission in Burma have left an indelible mark on history, reminding us of all that with faith, even the smallest acts of kindness and courage can change the world.

In the year of our Lord 1812, Judson set forth on a noble quest, departing from the embrace of his homeland into the spiritual wilderness of Burma. The cultural, linguistic, and spiritual chasms he encountered echoed the trials faced by Paul as he shared the gospel with both Jews and Gentiles. In a land steeped in the teachings of Buddhism, the path to Christianity was fraught with peril and scarcity. For six long years, much like Paul in his early days, Judson toiled without the visible fruits of his labor, holding steadfast to the belief that the seeds of God's Word would one day flourish.

Mirroring the sufferings of Paul—who endured beatings, imprisonment, and shipwreck—Judson's odyssey was fraught with tribulations. One of the darkest chapters of his life unfolded during the Anglo-Burmese War, when he was unjustly imprisoned, accused of espionage. In the grim shadows of a Burmese dungeon, shackled and tormented, Judson's faith faced its fiercest trials. Yet, akin to Paul, whose prison letters uplifted entire Christian communities, Judson emanated hope and resilience. His beloved wife, Ann, stood as a beacon of support during these dark times, reminiscent of the faithful companions who bolstered Paul's mission.

Just as Paul found joy even amid suffering, declaring, *"For to me, to live is Christ and to die is gain"* (Philippians 1:21), Judson's hardships deepened his dependence on

God and fortified his missionary spirit. After years of dedication, he celebrated a monumental triumph—baptizing his first Burmese convert, a breakthrough as momentous as Paul's mission to the Gentiles. By the close of his earthly journey, Judson had not only sown the seeds of Christianity throughout Burma but had also accomplished the monumental task of translating the Bible into Burmese—a legacy that resonates with the enduring power of Paul's epistles, which continue to nurture believers across generations.

For missionaries today, Judson's tale stands as a vibrant testament to the spirit of St. Paul. Both men exemplified that the cost of discipleship—whether through suffering, sacrifice, or even the ultimate price of death—is never in vain when undertaken for the glory of Christ and the expansion of His kingdom. Their lives beckon us to persevere in faith, viewing every challenge as a divine opportunity to magnify God's glory. With each step taken in faith, missionaries continue to draw strength from the legacies of Johnson and Paul, finding inspiration in their courage and unwavering dedication. Their stories encourage modern disciples to remain steadfast, nurturing the spiritual seeds planted through acts of love, humility, and service.

In today's ever-changing world, the essence of their mission remains unchanged: to bridge cultural divides with compassion, to communicate the message of love in a language that transcends words, and to foster communities rooted in hope and redemption. As we carry forward this sacred mission, we are reminded that the journey, though fraught with challenges, is also rich with the promise of transformation—for both the messenger and those who receive the message.

May the echoes of Judson's and Paul's missions resound in our hearts, inspiring us to walk boldly in their footsteps, fueled by the same divine purpose that guided them through every trial and triumph.

11

Ole Henry and Ahmed

Henry, a retired missionary in his eighties, has dedicated his post-retirement years to serving the community in a bustling urban neighborhood in Chicago. After years of impactful work in rural Africa, Henry returned to the United States with a burning desire to continue his mission of community building.

Driven by his passion for helping others, Henry started a soup kitchen from his garage. Every evening, he opens his doors to serve meals to the homeless population in the area. However, Henry's approach goes beyond mere charity. He views these meals to foster human connection and provide a sense of belonging to those in need.

One of Henry's remarkable qualities is his fluency in multiple languages, a skill gained during his missionary work. This linguistic ability allows him to communicate effectively with the diverse individuals who seek assistance at his soup kitchen. From immigrants and refugees to locals, Henry's welcoming demeanor and language proficiency create a welcoming atmosphere for all who come through his door.

Henry's selfless dedication to serving others exemplifies the power of compassion and community building. His soup kitchen not only provides nourishment for the body but also serves as a beacon of hope and unity in the heart of a bustling urban environment. Henry's unwavering commitment to creating human connections transcends barriers, making a lasting impact on all who cross his path.

On a frigid winter night, Henry, a retired missionary, crossed paths with Ahmed, a young man from Yemen who was struggling to navigate his new life in a foreign land. Ahmed, touched by Henry's kindness, revealed that he had been feeling isolated and hadn't spoken to anyone in weeks. This chance encounter led to a blossoming friendship as the two began meeting regularly. Henry took on the role of an English tutor for Ahmed, while Ahmed shared his culinary skills by teaching Henry how to cook traditional Yemeni dishes.

As their bond grew stronger, Ahmed's life took a positive turn. With Henry's guidance and support, Ahmed could secure a job and start building a new life for himself in his adopted country. In a heartwarming display of gratitude, Ahmed began volunteering at the local soup kitchen to pay it forward and help those in need, inspired by Henry's selfless acts of kindness.

Henry's story is a powerful reminder of how the spirit of service and connection knows no boundaries of age, nationality, or retirement status. Despite being in his later years, Henry continues to impact lives with his muted yet persistent acts of compassion. Through his friendship with Ahmed, Henry exemplifies the profound impact that a simple gesture of kindness can have on someone's life, transcending cultural differences and fostering a sense of unity and understanding in a diverse world.

The saying may be redundant, but here goes: "Salvation is one beggar telling another beggar where to find food." This simple yet profound statement encapsulates the essence of compassion, empathy, and humanity. It highlights the idea that those who have found salvation or solace in their lives have a duty to share that knowledge and support with others who are still struggling.

Just as a beggar in need of food would appreciate guidance from someone who has found sustenance, so too should we be willing to offer a helping hand to those in need. We uplift others and create a sense of community and interconnectedness by sharing our experiences, wisdom, and resources; this brings hope and healing to those who are lost or suffering.

In a world where kindness and generosity can sometimes seem scarce, the act of one beggar helping another serves as a powerful reminder of the transformative power of empathy and solidarity. This simple yet profound act highlights the beauty of human connection and compassion, breaking through barriers of societal norms and prejudices. It exemplifies the essence of our shared humanity and the potential we all must uplift each other in times of need.

As we navigate the complexities of life, let us all strive to be that guiding light for one another, leading by example and extending a helping hand. By fostering empathy and solidarity in our interactions, we create a ripple effect of positivity and support that can shape a more compassionate and inclusive society. Together, we can overcome challenges, bridge divides, and build a community based on understanding and mutual respect.

In embracing our collective responsibility to care for one another, we not only provide nourishment for the body and soul but also pave the way for a brighter future filled with hope and salvation. Let us cherish the moments of connection and unity that arise from acts of kindness, no matter how small, and let them inspire us to continue spreading love and compassion in a world that sorely needs it.

12

Faith and Missions

Faith deeply connects to missions, and numerous scriptures emphasize the call to reach out, serve, and share hope. Here are some significant ones, coupled with reflective thoughts that may resonate with your journey:

Matthew 28:19-20 (The Great Commission)

"Go therefore and make disciples of all nations, baptizing them in the name of the Father and of the Son and of the Holy Spirit, teaching them to observe all that I have commanded you. And behold, I am with you always, to the end of the age."

The foundational scripture emphasizes the universal and eternal call to missions—both near and far. It serves as a guiding light for missionaries as they step into unfamiliar lands or communities. Many missionaries have shared that these verses were their North Star, providing them with direction and purpose in their service.

The scripture highlights the importance of spreading the message of faith to all corners of the world, emphasizing the need for both local and global missions. It underscores the significance of reaching out to those in need, regardless of geographical boundaries. This call to missions transcends cultural barriers and time, urging believers to share the love and teachings of their faith with others.

The foundational scripture serves as a powerful reminder of the universal and eternal call to missions. It motivates missionaries to step out of their comfort zones and into unfamiliar territories, guided by the principles of faith and compassion. As a North Star for many, these verses inspire individuals to spread the message of love and hope to communities near and far.

Romans 10:13-15

"For everyone who calls on the name of the Lord will be saved. How, then, can they call on the one they have not believed in? And how can they believe in the one of whom they have not heard? And how can they hear without someone preaching to them? And how can anyone preach unless they are sent?"

Romans 10:13–15 is a profound passage that highlights the interconnectedness of salvation, faith, and the mission of sharing the gospel. Let's take it step by step and explore its deeper meaning:

Romans 10:13

"For everyone who calls on the name of the Lord will be saved."

This verse reveals the universal accessibility of salvation. The Lord saves anyone who calls on him, regardless of ethnicity, culture, or status. This powerful reminder urges everyone everywhere to receive the message of hope and redemption.

Romans 10:14

"How, then, can they call on the one they have not believed in? And how can they believe in the one of whom they have not heard? And how can they hear without someone preaching to them?"

This verse lays out the chain reaction of faith, highlighting the interconnected steps necessary for someone to call on the Lord. It emphasizes the pivotal role of believers in actively proclaiming the gospel and engaging in missions.

1. Calling on the Lord: The goal of the chain reaction is for individuals to call on the Lord, seeking salvation and guidance in their lives.

2. Believing: Prior to calling on the Lord, individuals must first believe in Him and His message. This belief serves as the foundation for their faith journey.

3. Hearing: Belief starts through hearing the message of the gospel. This underscores the importance of sharing the Good News with others.

4. Sharing the Message: Believers must actively share the gospel message with others. By doing so, they play a crucial role in initiating the chain reaction of faith in others.

This verse underscores the vital role of believers in actively proclaiming the gospel and engaging in missions to facilitate the chain reaction of faith. It serves as a reminder of the responsibility and privilege of sharing the message of salvation with others.

Romans 10:15

"And how can anyone preach unless they are sent? As it is written: 'How beautiful are the feet of those who bring good news!'"

Here, Paul celebrates the role of the sent ones—those who go out to share the Good News. The phrase "beautiful feet" symbolizes the honor and joy of bringing a life-changing message to others, no matter the effort or journey it requires.

Themes to Reflect On

The Necessity of Missions: This passage highlights that faith doesn't happen in isolation. It takes intentional effort to bridge the gap between those who know God and those who don't.

Partnership in the Gospel: The process described here involves a partnership—those who send, those who go, and those who receive. It's a shared mission within the body of Christ.

Urgency of the Message: The logical progression in this text underscores the urgency of sharing the gospel. Without it, many will not hear or believe.

This passage has deeply inspired many in the mission field. For instance, a missionary once shared how they clung to Romans 10:15 during a tough time in a remote village. It reminded them that their presence there, even with its challenges, was part of God's plan to reach people who hadn't yet heard His message.

On a more personal level, I've read about communities transformed through simple acts of preaching and service.

One pastor recounted how a single sermon in a small, forgotten town led to a ripple effect, as the locals began sharing the message themselves, turning their community into a hub of faith and hope.

Isaiah 6:8

"Then I heard the voice of the Lord saying, 'Whom shall I send? And who will go for us?' And I said, 'Here am I. Send me!'"

This is the eager response of a willing servant. I once heard a missionary describe how these words echoed in their heart when they were wrestling with leaving a comfortable life to follow God's call to serve overseas.

In that moment of divine calling, the missionary felt a deep sense of purpose and conviction. Despite the challenges and uncertainties that lay ahead, the missionary found courage and strength in the belief that they were answering a higher calling. The decision to leave behind familiarity and embark on a journey of faith was not an easy one, but it was driven by a profound sense of obedience and trust in God's plan.

As the missionaries reflected on their own journey of faith, they found solace in the words of Isaiah 6:8. It became a source of inspiration and a reminder of their willingness to say, "Here am I. Send me!" was a testament to their unwavering faith and commitment to serving the Lord. This scripture served as a guiding light, illuminating the path ahead and reaffirming their decision to follow God's call, wherever it may lead.

Acts 1:8

"But you will receive power when the Holy Spirit has come upon you; and you will be my witnesses in Jerusalem and in all Judea and Samaria, and to the end of the earth."
- Acts 1:8

Summary: This verse emphasizes the role of the Holy Spirit in empowering believers to be bold witnesses for Christ. It highlights the progression from local to global outreach, starting in Jerusalem and expanding to Judea, Samaria, and to the ends of the earth. The Holy Spirit provides the strength, courage, and guidance needed for effective witnessing, enabling believers to share the message of Christ with others in their communities and beyond.

John 20:21

"As the Father has sent me, I am sending you."

This short statement reminds us we are sent out into the world, just as Jesus was.

Personal Reflections

Missions often require stepping into the unknown, yet the reward is witnessing transformation—both in the lives of those served and in one's own heart. For instance, a pastor once shared how going on a short-term mission trip opened his eyes to the resilience and joy of a small rural community, even in their material lack. Their faith encouraged him to reframe his perspective on gratitude and provision.

Similarly, I've come across stories of everyday individuals—teachers, builders, medical professionals—who unexpectedly took part in missions. For one such person, it was reading the Great Commission while working their regular 9-to-5 job and realizing that "making disciples" could begin right at their workplace, long before heading to a distant land.

If you are interested in participating in a mission trip, then contact your local pastor, who will guide you in the right direction. Most major denominations have missionaries across the world who would love to host a mission team to help them strengthen their ministries. Become involved today and receive a bountiful blessing!

13

"Unto the Least" – Rev. Bobby Gale

My cherished friend in faith, the Rev. Bobby Gale, hailing from the charming city of Savannah, Georgia, embarked on a noble ministry many years ago, reaching out to the hearts of Uganda, Ghana, the Democratic Republic of Congo, and beyond. During a fateful journey to this vibrant land, he unearthed a pressing need for wells to be created across various communities, granting them the precious gift of fresh and clean water. Until then, the villagers had drawn from murky puddles and drainage ditches, leading to a cascade of afflictions that plagued their lives. Alas, the little ones withstood the worst of this suffering, their spirits dimmed by the weight of illness.

Determined to make a meaningful difference, Rev. Gale rallied support from both near and far, weaving a tapestry of compassion and generosity. With the help of dedicated volunteers and the contributions of kind-hearted individuals, the project took shape. Each well that was drilled not only quenched the physical thirst of the villagers but also rekindled hope and joy within their hearts. He officially named his mission, "Unto the Least of His." (www.untotheleast.com or bobby@totheleast.com)

The communities gathered to celebrate the arrival of clean water, their songs of gratitude echoing through the lush landscapes. Children, once weakened by disease, now danced with newfound energy, their laughter a testament to the transformative power of Rev. Gale's mission and vision. This endeavor not only improved health but also fostered education, as children could now attend school regularly instead of spending hours fetching water.

Through his unwavering commitment and the collective efforts of many, Rev. Gale's vision became a reality, illustrating that even the smallest acts of kindness can ripple outwards to create profound change. His legacy continues to inspire others to look beyond borders and see the shared humanity that binds us all.

In the years following the establishment of the wells, the community thrived in ways previously unimaginable. Gardens blossomed with vibrant fruits and vegetables, nourished by the clean water that now flowed freely. The villagers, invigorated by the health and opportunity this water brought, explored new avenues for growth and development. Small businesses emerged, powered by the newfound availability of water, which fueled not only agriculture but also craftsmanship and trade.

Rev. Gale's mission sparked a broader movement, encouraging other communities and organizations to take similar steps in addressing water scarcity across the globe. Educators conducted workshops, teaching sustainable practices and the importance of water conservation, thus securing these precious resources for future generations.

The story of "Unto the Least of His" became a beacon of hope, a reminder that one person's dream, when shared and nurtured by many, could indeed change the world. Visitors from everywhere came to witness the transformation, leaving with hearts full of inspiration and a renewed belief in the power of collective action. The wells stood as symbols of unity and resilience, monuments to the enduring spirit of compassion and the unyielding belief in a better tomorrow.

I have lost track of the many wells that Bobby has brought to life in Africa and beyond, all thanks to the boundless generosity of his numerous benefactors here in the States. With unwavering enthusiasm, Bobby forges ahead, never accepting "no" as a definitive answer. When one possesses the will, they can truly transform the world.

Thank you, Bobby, for being a cherished friend. Our hearts overflow with love for you, as do God's. Your tireless dedication has not only provided essential resources but has also inspired countless others to join the cause of uplifting those in need. Your journey reminds us that change is possible when driven by love and compassion. The ripples of your efforts have touched lives in ways that words alone cannot capture, creating a legacy that will endure for generations.

May your work continue to flourish, and may you find joy knowing that you have made a significant difference in the lives of so many. Your story is a testament to the incredible power of human kindness and the profound impact one person can have when they choose to act with purpose and heart.

**Bobby's ministry is based on Matthew 25:40: "Inasmuch as ye have done it unto one of the least of these my brethren, ye have done it unto me."

14

"One Small Step for Man"

"That's one small step for man, one giant leap for mankind." - Neil Armstrong, Apollo 11 Moon Landing.

On July 20, 1969, astronaut Neil Armstrong became the first human to set foot on the surface of the moon during the Apollo 11 mission. This historic event marked a significant milestone in human history, highlighting the incredible achievements of space exploration and the advancements of science and technology. Neil Armstrong's iconic words, "That's one small step for man, one giant leap for mankind," captured the essence of this momentous occasion, symbolizing the collective progress and ambition of humanity.

As missionaries dedicated to the pursuit of new horizons and possibilities for humanity, we approach quotes such as the one provided with utmost seriousness. This quote encapsulates the essence of our ultimate mission: strapping ourselves into a spacecraft and embarking on a journey into the unknown territories of space. Just like pioneers venturing into uncharted territory, we are driven by a sense of exploration and discovery, fueled by the desire to push the boundaries of human knowledge and achievement. Our mission is not just a physical journey but a spiritual and intellectual one, where we seek to unlock the mysteries of the universe and pave the way for a brighter future for all humanity.

"In the end, we will remember not the words of our enemies, but the silence of our friends." - Martin Luther King Jr.

Friendship is a powerful bond that shapes our lives and influences our memories. Martin Luther King Jr.'s poignant words remind us of the impact of silence on our relationships. When our friends choose to remain silent in times of adversity, their absence of support can leave an impression. This quote serves as a powerful reminder to speak up for what is right and to stand by our friends when they need us the most. Let us cherish the voices of our friends and strive to never let silence define our relationships.

In a world filled with darkness and despair, it is our calling to shine brightly as beacons of light. This calling reminds us of the importance of spreading love, hope, and the message of Christ to all people. Through missions, we strive to build friendships, cultivate connections, and share the transformative power of God's love.

Our mission as believers is not merely to exist within the confines of our own faith communities, but to actively engage the world. By reaching out to others, we can break down barriers, foster understanding, and show the inclusive nature of Christ's love. Amid uncertainty and turmoil, our role as beacons of light becomes even more vital. We are called to offer a guiding light in the darkness, showing compassion, empathy, and solidarity with those in need.

Through missions, we have the privilege of connecting with people from diverse backgrounds and cultures. By building genuine friendships and relationships, we can share the love of Christ in a tangible and meaningful way.

Our actions speak louder than words, and by embodying the values of compassion, kindness, and acceptance, we can truly make a difference in the lives of others.

As we embrace our mission to be beacons of light in a shadowy world, let us remember the profound impact of our actions. Through missions, we can reflect the love of Christ to all people, regardless of their beliefs or backgrounds. By extending a hand of friendship and sharing the message of hope, we can truly make a difference in the world. Let us continue to shine brightly, illuminating the path for others and spreading the light of God's love wherever we go.

"The best way to find yourself is to lose yourself in the service of others." - Mahatma Gandhi

Service to others has the remarkable ability to not only benefit those being served but also to provide a path for self-discovery and personal growth. When we dedicate ourselves to helping others, we often find that we uncover hidden strengths, develop empathy, and compassion, and gain a deeper understanding of ourselves and the world. Mahatma Gandhi's words serve as a powerful reminder that by selflessly giving to others, we can find our true purpose and identity. Let us embrace the transformative power of service to not only make a difference in the lives of others but also to embark on a journey of self-discovery and fulfillment.

"Alone we can do so little; together, we can do so much." - Helen Keller

Collaboration is a fundamental aspect of human achievement. This quote by Helen Keller highlights the importance of working together towards a common goal. When individuals come together, their collective efforts can lead to remarkable accomplishments that would not have been possible alone. Collaboration fosters creativity, innovation, and synergy, allowing diverse perspectives and skills to complement each other. By pooling resources and expertise, teams can overcome challenges, solve complex problems, and achieve remarkable success. Helen Keller's words serve as a reminder of the transformative power of collaboration in both personal and professional endeavors. "Alone, we can do so little; together, we can do so much." - Helen Keller

Mission Briefing:

Welcome, Agent Cravey.

We have selected you for a highly classified and crucial mission. Your skills, expertise, and dedication have made you the ideal candidate for this assignment. The success of this mission is of utmost importance and will have far-reaching implications.

Mission Objective:

Your primary objective is to secure new disciples for Jesus Christ in the country of Nicaragua. This task will require precision, stealth, and quick thinking. The success of this mission rests solely on your shoulders.

Mission Parameters:

You are to operate under the highest level of secrecy and discretion. Any breach of protocol could jeopardize the entire operation. Trust no one except for your fellow agents and maintain constant vigilance.

Mission Timeline:

Time is of the essence. You are required to complete this mission within ten days. Failure to meet the deadline could have disastrous consequences for the lost.

Mission Acceptance:

By accepting this document, you acknowledge the importance of this mission and your commitment to its success. Your actions will determine the outcome, and the future depends on your dedication and resolve.

This document will self-destruct in 5...4...3...2...1...

Imagine a call to you to be a team member on a mission somewhere. Would you be open to going? Would you seriously pray about it and answer "yes" to God? The missions are just this serious.

"We choose to go to the moon in this decade and do the other things, not because they are easy, but because they are hard." - John F. Kennedy

In his historic speech delivered on September 12, 1962, President John F. Kennedy articulated the ambitious goal of sending American astronauts to the moon before the end of the 1960s. Emphasizing the importance of tackling challenges that require innovation, determination, and hard work, Kennedy inspired a nation to pursue the extraordinary feat of space exploration. This speech marked a pivotal moment in the space race between the United States and the Soviet Union, propelling the American space program towards unprecedented advancements in technology and science. Kennedy's vision and leadership laid the foundation for the successful Apollo missions that eventually landed humans on the moon.

Just as important are our missions to other nations, societies, and individuals who need to hear about the saving grace of Jesus Christ.

"Failure is not an option." - Associated with Gene Kranz, NASA Flight Director during the Apollo 13 mission.

During the intense moments of the Apollo 13 mission, Gene Kranz uttered these powerful words, encapsulating the unwavering determination and resilience required when faced with insurmountable challenges. Kranz's leadership and commitment to problem-solving under pressure have become emblematic of the human spirit's ability to overcome adversity. This quote serves as a reminder that, in times of crisis, giving up is never an option. Instead, it is a call to action to persevere, innovate, and push the boundaries of what is possible. The legacy of Gene Kranz and the Apollo 13 mission continue to inspire individuals and organizations worldwide to confront challenges head-on and strive for success against all odds.

Our mission programs are just as important to our recipients. People are hurting to hear God's word. We must go into the world to share it.

In the iconic movie Star Wars: The Empire Strikes Back, the wise Jedi Master Yoda imparts a profound lesson with his famous quote: **"Do or do not. There is no try."** This powerful statement encapsulates the essence of determination and commitment, emphasizing the importance of fully committing to one's actions without hesitation or doubt. Yoda's words serve as a reminder to embrace a mindset of decisiveness and confidence in pursuing our goals and aspirations. In a galaxy far, far away, these words continue to inspire and resonate with audiences of all ages, transcending the boundaries of fiction to impart timeless wisdom.

Each of these quotes captures the essence of determination, aspiration, and courage in the face of challenges. They were tailor made for missionaries who give themselves willingly to serve Christ. May we go with passion to serve wherever God calls us.

15

A Call to Mission

Amid the symphony of bustling streets,
A gentle voice, a heartbeat beats.
It whispers softly, yet so bright,
"A world in need, draw ever near, with light."

Through shadowed alleys and mountains high,
Where sorrows linger and shadows sigh,
A hand reaches forth, a beacon glows,
No heart forgotten, no soul alone, it knows.

Across the vast seas, where cultures embrace,
In languages rare, in warm, kind faces,

The mission flows like rivers of grace,
Uniting spirits in every space.

It's not the grand, the loud, the proud,
But tender whispers that weave through the crowd.
A cup of water, a warming smile,
The footsteps of love that traverse each mile.

Oh, missions, not merely tasks confined,
But in the love that binds humankind,
To heal, to teach, to mend, to guide,
To walk with others, side by side.

So let this tale forever bloom.
Like seeds of hope in a sunlit room,
And through the fields of time and space,
A mission's mark—a gift of grace.

Charles E. Cravey, 2025

16

A Seed of Hope

I lingered in stillness, hesitant to begin.
A quaking spirit, a heart held within.
The expanse beyond, so grand, so wide,
Could I, a mere seed, truly thrive?

Their whispers beckoned, "Come witness, come feel,
The echoes of souls, both distant and real."
Yet doubt, like shackles, confined my will,
Could I spark change? Could I fulfill?

Still, step by step, the path unveiled,
Each hand I grasped made my fears curtailed.

The weight dispersed, the sorrow released,
A battle fought, yet not just by least.

In shadowed streets, a child's bright grin,
In lands unknown, each journey's spin,
I discovered a truth, deep and profound—
That giving uplifts where sorrow surrounds.

It's not the might we believe we miss,
But courage found in each earnest kiss.
A life once cloaked in timid gloom,
Now strides in light where love finds bloom.

So here I stand, both daring and meek,
A humble answer to the call I seek.
For in this mission, our hearts entwine,
And purpose flourishes in yours and mine.

Charles E. Cravey, 2025

17

In Memoriam: Jamie Gibson

Jamie Gibson was a beloved comrade and fellow seeker of adventure in our shared quest. For countless years, we traversed the globe together, accompanied by teams united in purpose. Jamie's spirit radiated with an infectious enthusiasm for every new destination, tirelessly rallying support to fund our next expedition! She thrived in the grand tapestry that extended beyond her own life, always eager to lend a hand and heed the call wherever our journeys led.

Eventually, Jamie embarked on a mission to Haiti, a land beset by poverty and illness. She contracted Hepatitis B in Haiti. The hospital swiftly admitted her for treatment upon her return. I had the bittersweet honor of visiting her just days before her departure from this world, my heart heavy at the sight of her plight. A steadfast soldier of the cross, Jamie was unwavering in her dedication to her missions. Rather than dwell on her own condition, she shared with me the profound impact of her journey and what it meant to her. A few days later, Jamie slipped away quietly, but the countless lives she illuminated across the globe will forever carry her memory in their hearts!

www.ingramcontent.com/pod-product-compliance
Lightning Source LLC
Chambersburg PA
CBHW051345040426
42453CB00007B/419